The Ogress of

Reading

By

Eithne Cullen

New Generation Publishing

My thanks to Declan Cullen, for his support in everything, along with Erin, Ian and Thomas Cullen who encourage me and thanks to Barbara Nadel for her guidance.

Real People, Real Stories

This book has been produced with assistance from
The London Borough of Barking and Dagenham
Library Service
Pen to Print: Real People, Real Stories Creative
Writing Project 2016
with funding from The Arts Council, England
Grants for the Arts.

The old baby farmer, the wretched Miss Dyer

At the Old Bailey her wages is paid.

In times long ago, we'd 'a' made a big fy-er

And roasted so nicely that wicked old jade.

(popular ballad)

Chapter One: The evidence

April 1896

There was only one way to be sure he'd catch her: if she had any hint that the police were closing in, he knew she'd bolt. It was a pattern, she'd had so many changes of name and changes of address it had, in the past, kept the police one step behind. "This time, this time..." Anderson told himself. They had one piece of evidence to launch their case but needed to catch her in her home to secure a conviction. She'd soon know if anyone was watching her house, she'd find out if people were asking questions; the very nature of baby farming depended on secrets and turning the other way when something was going on. She had to open the door to them herself; she had to invite them in. There was one sure way of making that happen.

Working with Sergeant James and the two constables they'd been assigned, Anderson kept a very low-profile watch on the house on Kensington Road. Anderson became angry with himself every time he thought of the raid on Piggotts Road - arriving too late, finding nothing to connect the missing occupants with the parcels they'd had dragged from the water in the lock. The neighbours had been no help either, using words like "genteel" and "refined" to talk about her. They'd told him she did nothing to excite suspicion, the hollow words rankled with him. Nothing to excite suspicion, in a world that punished young women for giving birth, where hungry girls were preyed on by so called respectable types – he had to catch this woman, put an end to her vile practices.

With a new address to concentrate on, they had to get this right and not give her the chance to add yet another address, another alias to her already full repertoire of homes and identities. They needed to be vigilant; the main aim of their surveillance had to be to prevent her flitting in the night.

As he and James went over the plan of action, the solution was glaringly obvious. They would use a possible victim to gain access to the house. They'd set up a business prospect for Dyer, knowing full well it wasn't in her nature to miss an opportunity. Always scheming and dealing, she was forever looking for ways to earn money and entrap the weak. He needed a young woman to act as a decoy who would go to the old midwife for help and advice. She'd ask: "What's to become of my child?" The workhouse was close to Dyer's house and he and James found someone not too scared to play the role. She was in the family way herself, a thin woman in a shabby coat, her skin pale and stretched over a troubled face. Her name was Evie.

Within a week, "Mrs Thomas" had received an enquiry from a fallen woman looking for a home for her coming child. Dyer's instructions were clear, she was to raise ten pounds and put together some clothes and linen for the child. She was told to call on Good Friday, a quiet morning with little going on in the road apart from church goers on their way to the long services.

The trap was set. And there they were, on that crisp spring morning. Anderson felt guilty when he saw his team all there; they should have been at home, too, getting ready for the holy feast. They told him they'd seen the daughter, Mrs Palmer, setting out with her basket a little while ago. He knew she'd be off to the bakers to do her Good Friday shopping. The bakers' ovens were on this morning, for the last time until after they'd celebrated the Resurrection. It was traditional to get bread for the weekend and buy the cakes and buns for the Easter meal. Lent had been arduous, people had gone without their treats and sweet things for forty days and they'd break their fast after church tomorrow night. Anderson could almost smell the bun spices; he knew the cheeky bakers sprinkled them on the doorsteps to entice their customers to buy. He knew that his own mother would be out, now, collecting the Good Friday eggs. When she'd brought them in she'd mark each one with a cross, to make their Easter eggs for Sunday breakfast. He remembered the joy, as a boy, of being allowed to eat three or even four boiled eggs for his breakfast – on a normal Sunday one would have been a treat, sometimes he'd share one with his brother. He'd be eating them again this Easter day and he'd hug his mother and wish her blessings.

Heavily, his thoughts came back to the opposite of motherly love, the death-dealing murderer. They had to stop her before she had a chance to dispose of any incriminating evidence.

The tall, uniformed men looked at their superior, quizzically, awaiting the nod. He signalled a yes and muttered their instructions. One straight upstairs, one to the garden - to look for signs of recently turned soil - they knew the sort of thing. Evie straightened her hat, smoothed down her shabby coat and looked to him. He nodded calmly, reassuringly. She knocked and the front door opened to let her in. She stepped back to allow Inspector Anderson to come face to face with the killer.

He was surprised to see the woman who'd been his obsession for so long, whom he categorised as beast, ogress, murderer there in front of him. She was a tall woman but she was heavy set. She wore a shabby black dress and stained apron. He looked into her lined face, flabby-cheeked and pasty. He'd expected to see a monster but saw an unexceptional figure. The look of puzzlement on her face lasted only a few seconds. She knew, she realised and she stepped back to let him in. It was almost as if she'd been expecting him, expecting them to raid this little terraced house. The look that passed between them was not remarkable, but he'd remember this moment, this look of recognition. In years to come, he'd tell people how the Ogress of Reading had welcomed him into her house with a look of passive resignation on her face.

Sergeant James and the officers went in before him. Evie turned and walked back along the street towards the workhouse and the hopeless future she knew she had to face. Maybe "Mrs Thomas" could have helped her, even changed her life? Anderson would go and see her later, see how he could help her out of her situation, perhaps his mother...

"Mrs Thomas?"

She just pulled the door wider to let him in.

"Mrs Thomas. Do you recognise this? "He held the paper from the parcel, his only substantive piece of evidence. She barely looked at it.

His voice took on a sharper edge, a more forthright tone: "Mrs Thomas, or should I say Amelia Dyer? Have you seen this paper before? Do you know how it has come to be in police possession?"

Her nod conceded that she knew the parcel.

Her crumpled face took on a bewildered look or perhaps she was looking right through him. The voice, when it came out, surprised him. It wasn't the voice of a terrible murderer, but the sound of someone's grandma, reedy and soft. No wonder she'd taken in so many desperate young women.

"I do not know anything about it; it's all a mystery to me."

Stepping back, she let Anderson pass her and enter the house.

The smell hit him straight away. He knew it well. He knew he'd find sour milk in the jug he spotted on the table, putrid butter in a dish, rotting vegetables in a basket somewhere. It was a smell of decay and it turned his stomach and brought bile to his throat.

This was the odour of decomposition, he'd smelt it when he'd found bodies that had lain undiscovered in the alleys or fields around Reading; he'd smelt it when they'd

4

had to move corpses from shallow graves at the edge of the woods; he'd smelt it when they'd had to exhume graves for courts to enquire into macabre crimes and he'd smelt this smell when they'd raided the surgeon's house where illegal dissection lessons had been taking place. He fully expected to find human remains here, in this house and was astonished not to find them there at all.

He scanned the room, taking in the mess. While he and his men had been closing in, the woman was sitting in a house filled with evidence, enough, he hoped, to take her to the gallows. Dyer was shocked, speechless. Her son-in-law, Arthur Palmer was sitting by the fire, staring in disbelief at the scene that was unfolding before him. Anderson gave the nod to James, who took him out and placed him under arrest. An older woman, they knew was called Jane Smith, sat silently at the other side of the hearth clutching some knitting to her chest, her mouth had fallen open in shock and remained open for the rest of their visit.

The worn carpet, threadbare in places, was marked with all kinds of grubby stains; he'd get Harris to examine it for blood or any other incriminating clue. In the corner was a box, a packing case made from flimsy board. Looking inside it he saw that it had been lined with rags. It could easily have been a cot or cradle for an infant. Stuffed in the corner behind it, tumbled in a pile, he saw more material and was sure he'd find children's clothes in there.

There was a vase of blown yellow roses next to the rancid butter in its dish. Their deathly pose and wilted, shrivelled petals made him shudder. The roses decaying in their green, slimy water summed up the room for him: the loss, the waste. Anderson thought of the brackish water where the bodies had been found, stagnant pools of green, like the water in the vase.

Further along the table, lay a soft tobacco pouch. Anderson lifted it and heard the grisly rattle that told him it held pills. Peering in, he saw an assortment of small white and yellow tablets, a random mix of death dealing fare. Before he put the pouch back, his eye was drawn to a little pile of papers, dockets, which he recognised straight away. He hoped this might be the evidence he could finally use, to confirm his suspicions about this evil woman. They were pawn shop tickets, on rough paper, neatly torn. He lifted the pile and read the first. It was for a small sum, he couldn't read the numbers, three or five shillings for a baby's dress and bonnet, linen, white. It could be the evidence he needed. Surely some mother could confirm that these were clothes she'd bought for her own child. Anderson knew, felt it in his heart, he'd got her. He had what he had come for.

The search continued and he was astonished to see that she had kept letters from mothers she'd dealt with. These sad missives stirred his emotions; he read the words of women who enquired after their children's well being and development. Children who had probably only lived long enough for the letters to arrive; letters that had always gone unanswered and never given the reassurances they were looking for. Rummaging through the pile, he saw more, equally incriminating papers. Here were telegrams with times and dates clearly set out for the handover of children for adoption. He'd use these to help determine the cases they knew little about or could not prove to be her crimes. There were receipts from the local newspapers she'd used to advertise her trade, papers from Reading, London and Bristol. Mentally, Anderson was able to join the dots on the map in his head. There was even a certificate recording the vaccination that had been administered to one of the children. One of the mothers had tried to prevent her infant dying from small pox, while Dyer killed - poison for some, strangling for others.

Anderson was surprised to hear the movement of the other officers in the room. He'd almost forgotten them.

"Take her into custody." He called to James, "Put her in the wagon with her son-in-law."

As James began to move, he added: "Any sign of the daughter?"

"Not yet."

"Look out for her and take her in as well. Try to get her before she realises what's happening, maybe get them to move the wagon down the road a way."

James left with Dyer; who hastily took a shawl to put around her shoulders. Now, she looked more like some helpless old lady. He cast the image from his mind.

Harris came down from the upper floor; he asked him, "Anything?"

Harris told him there were some clothes and an empty trunk under the bed, this also smelt rotten. He'd brought down Dyer's mending basket and handed it to Anderson. The detective asked him to go through the piles in the corner and Harris began to unravel dresses, shawls and little vests from the tangle, probably not worth pawning but still held on to. Anderson thought of Evie, who'd be able to use all this.

James returned to tell him they'd now got the daughter in the wagon. They'd finish looking here, then seal up the house until Monday. He called out to all three: "Almost done, now, thanks men." Then, to James, "Take the wagon to the police station; you might as well wait there."

Out in the little yard behind the house, a constable called Gale was still looking for recently turned earth, although all he'd found was some caterpillar-chewed greens and a row of potatoes. They had all thought they'd find some bodies or other evidence there, but it made sense, if the family was always on the move, they would not want to leave anything behind.

"When you've finished there, see if you can pick up anything from that rug, please." Anderson would get his men home shortly, back to their families and their holiday.

Turning his attention to the sewing basket, he found socks for darning, little scraps of ribbon and lace, needles and pins, sharp scissors and thimbles. Down at the bottom,

7

he felt a roll of stuff. He pulled it out and recognised it, white edging tape, the same tape she'd used to strangle the babies they'd found in the river. He shuddered at the thought of the tape in his hand being tied twice around the neck of a child and secured with a knot.

He stopped what he was doing and called to his officers: "Enough! We've found enough!"

Chapter 2: Childhood

1838-

Pyle Marsh was a small village a few miles east of Bristol. Sarah and Samuel Hobley made their home there and lived comfortably with their little family. Samuel was a successful man - a master shoemaker attracting customers who wanted quality shoes along with the constant demand for hard-wearing boots for the villagers. They had five children, sturdy boys Thomas, James and William and two little girls, Sarah Ann and Amelia. Samuel provided well for them and was adamant they should all learn to read and write and make their way in the world. He paid a weekly fee for his daughters to go to the church school; some of the small number of girls who were able to keep attending until the age of fourteen.

As the youngest, Amelia was always included in her siblings' games. She tagged along to watch the boys wrestle and jostle over some ball or chase game and she and Sarah Ann played girlish games in the fields while the boys played around them. They had dolls made from wooden pegs which they arranged in rows for their lessons and they set up home among the ferns, displaying broken bits of china as if they were the most expensive ornaments in the world. Their mother, Sarah, worked hard running the home and looking after her family. It was difficult for a woman in those days, all the domestic chores fell to her and she had to enlist the help of all the children to do the housework. They had to black the range, whiten the doorstep, polish the brass and make up the fires before they went to their lessons or off to play. The boys were destined to learn trades; Thomas would inherit the shoe business, the others would work as carpenters and cabinet makers. Their parents made sure they did not experience the poverty so many children were forced to endure.

Like all families then, there were tragic moments, too. Amelia was devastated to lose her lovely sister, who died of typhus fever at the age of six, leaving Amelia the only girl in this noisy family. She felt the loss of her close playmate keenly. Her mother, who had also been affected by the typhus had survived the illness but struggled for the rest of her life with mental problems as a result.

When Amelia was eight years old, she heard talk that there was to be another baby and longed for a sister. In this little cottage, there were few secrets and she watched her mother grow bigger with her child. Sure enough, a baby girl arrived; she was also given the name Sarah Ann. Amelia fussed around her mother and the baby. She was happy to hold and clean her and not shy to take her to her mother to feed. She seemed to be a natural nursemaid and little mother herself. The whole family was stunned when the little baby sickened and grew weak. She failed to thrive, lost weight and slipped away from them. Amelia's brothers thought it was strange that their little sister washed and laid the baby out. She heard their whispers "It's too much" they said and "a little girl should not have to deal with this kind of thing." She fussed over little Sarah Ann before she was taken off for burial. Already established as her mother's principal helper, Amelia took on the role more and more. She still kept up with her studies and escaped from the household chores by reading poetry and literature, which she loved.

Amelia also took note of her mother's erratic behaviour and outbursts. At such times, her mother's face would become distorted and her speech slurred and there were moments of hysteria when she was clearly hallucinating. Following these outbursts, she would seem to withdraw into quiet calm. Little Amelia soothed her through her violent fits and cared for her as well as she could. By the time she was eleven years old, she knew a great deal about the behaviour of the mentally ill. At times, Sarah had a stay in the new mental institution built near their home. When she came home she appeared to be better, she even seemed to be behaving normally. Again, it fell to the little girl to deal with her mother's outbursts and nurse her when she was feverish or distressed. She heard her brothers, again, whispering among themselves: "It's too much" they said and "a little girl should not have to deal with this kind of thing." Her brothers and father had nothing to offer, no way to ease the sick woman's suffering. They had to trust people then called "mad doctors" who treated the suffering of the mentally ill by calming them, often with opiates, until they became quiet and manageable. Amelia watched and learned a lot.

Sarah eventually died in a fitful, raving state. Her family was deeply affected. Samuel Hobley was left with children to care for along with a business to run. He could not stop his sad young family becoming quarrelsome. Amelia did what she could to keep the house running as it had before but there was strain and friction in the family. Her father knew she was a girl moving towards womanhood, still missing a woman's touch. He tried to talk to her but did not have the words. He told her he knew how to prepare the boys for their future lives, sorting out apprenticeships and jobs for them. Often he looked, wordlessly at his daughter and shook his head sadly. He could not fill the gap left by his wife's death. He had no idea how to bring up his daughter, how to deal with the changes she experienced in her body or the troubles she experienced in her mind.

He did not consult Amelia when he arranged for her to move away to stay with an aunt. It was a *fait accompli*. She found herself packed and moved to a house in Bristol, in a bustling street which was nothing like the home she had left. She learned the harsh lesson of separation without a chance to say goodbye or even to ask her father what was in his mind. Maybe, in later life, she remembered the cold of loss and separation and remembered how to harden herself against the hurt they caused. She learned first hand how a parent can give a child over to another.

Whether she was pleased with the move or not, she stayed with her aunt for a long time. She did not go home after that and was forced to become more independent and make her own way in the world. In fact, as she grew up, she had less and less contact with her brothers and eventually became estranged from them. Even when her father, Samuel, died from bronchitis she did not return to the family home. There was no reason, now, for Amelia to return to Pyle Marsh.

Totterdown, where her aunt lived, was a busy area of Bristol and was very different from the village she had grown up in. Amelia saw families living in crowded conditions in the bustling market area of the growing city. The railways had come and brought new workers and new housing as the town grew. She saw children whose lives were very different from the childhood she had known. She saw poverty and hunger. Her aunt gave her a home and there was no reason for her to be unhappy. It was a comfortable place but there was no real warmth there and none of the playful friendliness she remembered from her childhood. Her aunt was kind and helpful. Amelia had her own room, regular mealtimes and passed quiet evenings with her aunt and uncle reading or sewing in their neat parlour. She went to church with them and walked in the park with other young people after the service. But Amelia was not a child any more, so her aunt asked her about her future wanting to know what she wanted to do.

"Do, Aunt? I have never thought of it, can't I go along as I am?"

"Surely you must want to learn or study, or go to work and learn a trade, don't you?" Her Aunt replied.

"I've never thought about it, Aunt, my life was so much different when Mother was alive, I helped to run the house and cared for her when she was sick. What is there to do now?"

"I suppose we could keep you here until you marry, but it's not enough for a woman, Amelia, you cannot stay a child forever."

"I don't know as I shall ever marry, I do not know any men who could make good husbands."

Her aunt laughed at her matter-of-fact delivery of this line; she retold it often to her husband and friends. The poor girl looked so puzzled, at the notion she would have to go and find work or worthwhile employment for herself.

"As for work, I suppose I could make myself useful and find a trade for myself." She'd said.

"Let me talk to your uncle," her aunt said "I'm sure he can find out what would be the right thing for you to do."

Amelia's aunt and uncle looked into the possibilities of work for this bright, young woman and arranged for her to begin an apprenticeship in the corsetry trade.

By now, Amelia was a tall, strapping figure of a girl with exceptionally large hands and feet. She enjoyed the irony that she was making corsets for ladies to nip in already tiny waists and force their bodies into bird-like postures. However, she was a good worker and learned her trade well. She finished her apprenticeship and continued working there for quite some time. Each day she returned to her aunt's house, and continued to live quietly. She had made some friendships and was happier in herself. She stayed living with her aunt until she was twenty-four.

She met George Thomas while living at her aunt's house. It was an unlikely friendship, mainly because of the difference in their ages: Thomas was nearer sixty than fifty and Amelia was still in her early twenties. He was a prosperous man, who had earned his living as a gilder and carver, a highly respected professional. At the time he met Amelia, he lived with his grown-up son and his family, in a much more affluent area of the city. It had not been long since the death of his wife.

Amelia, who felt the time had come to move on, decided to leave her aunt's house and take a room in Trinity Street, Bristol. The house was run by a landlady who provided rooms and meals for paying guests. She kept a clean house, washed her lodgers' clothes and made sure it was a respectable establishment, with male and female boarders. Amelia settled there and continued her work at the corset factory. She was the perfect picture of a young, working woman, coming and going in her smart business-like fashion with her distinctive way of walking and her head held high.

No one spotted the coincidence when George Thomas moved in or wondered why a well-off man with a good home chose to live in lodgings. He and Amelia grew closer, their relationship grew stronger and they were married very soon. It was a quiet ceremony without any family present. Perhaps they were afraid of the reactions of their families when they married? Maybe Amelia thought George's son would think she was after his father's fortune? It was still only five months since his wife had died. So they went ahead with their wedding, quietly and privately. They filled in their details on their marriage certificate and, for some reason, decided to change the age difference between them: George shaved off ten years, recording his age as forty-eight while Amelia added on six years, claiming to be thirty. They began their married life and Amelia left her past behind her.

Chapter 3: A new profession

1863-

Being married to George brought many changes to Amelia's life. She had missed her father when she moved to Bristol and, although they had not been close for a very long time, was saddened by his death. Her memories of her childhood were of a hardworking father, more stable than his wife, who looked out for the interests of his daughter. She understood why he had sent her away, even if she had not liked it at the time. Now, here she was married to a man who could give her the comfort she longed for and the affection that had been missing for most of her adult life. They settled into married life.

At this time the profession of nursing was booming. There were opportunities for educated women like Amelia to receive high quality training and join this growing field. George's comfortable position meant that Amelia could train as a nurse while he supported her. "Go ahead, "he had said, "make the life you want for yourself."

She joined the Bristol Royal Infirmary's very first team of trainee nurses. During her training she experienced medical and surgical wards, gained an understanding of general medicine and midwifery and was given responsibility. Sometimes there would only be one nurse on duty, in charge of the wards on her own; it was hard and tiring work. Nurses were not seen as having medical expertise which belonged to the doctors and physicians; nurses cared for patients on long twelve-hour shifts and needed physical strength and resilience to deal with their sick and needy patients. With so many of the sick and poor needing help, the hospital was over-crowded and the nurses needed to be able to deal with rooms full of waiting patients. Amelia had the physical stature and strength to take this in her stride; she also showed the emotional strength and understanding that meant she did not cave in under the pressure of the job. Her experience of dealing with her mother's illness meant she was able to deal with most situations. Nursing was a profession that suited her well.

George was proud of her and supported her in her work. He understood the stresses she experienced doing long shifts and exhausting work. Even when Amelia fell pregnant at the age of twenty-seven, she wanted to carry on working. She kept her pregnancy hidden as long as she could and her large frame helped with this. However, a time came when she could no longer conceal it. She was called in by the authorities and told, as women were in those days, that she would have to leave the hospital. Amelia left to take on her role as a full time wife and mother. She gave birth to a baby girl who she called Ellen.

George was well off and able to support his wife and child. However, it was strange for him to have a new baby in the house, especially as his own children were grown with children their own. He saw Amelia raising the child, using her nursing skills and common sense to keep her healthy and thriving. Infant death was rife in those times; there were all kinds of infections and illnesses which the little ones could not fight. He was proud of Amelia and the way she was looking after them both.

Though Amelia did not keep in touch with many of her family members, there were often visitors to the house. One of these was a relation of George's, a distant cousin from Southport, who was moving to Bristol. She was also a nurse, moving to the city to set up a business looking after women during their confinement. While she was waiting to move into her new house, she stayed with the Thomas family. She was also called Ellen and the two women laughed at the coincidence. She and Amelia would spend long periods engrossed in conversation and George saw that they were talking about nursing and childcare, he was happy that they had met and made this friendship.

What George did not know or suspect, was that the conversation often took a sinister tone. While he nodded benignly in his chair after supper, he thought they were talking about the secrets of reproduction. He did not know that Ellen Dane was telling Amelia of the business she ran in what was widely known as "baby farming." She explained to Amelia that she ran a lying-in home for women at the end of their pregnancies. Often they would be keeping their pregnancy secret. There was a huge stigma attached to pregnancy outside of marriage. "Women in trouble" would come to Dane when they could no longer keep it a secret. She would provide them with a place to stay, look after their health and deliver their babies when the time came. Some of those new mothers' confinements were quite long. They would only leave when they were ready. It all seemed very straightforward. Amelia could see it was a way for Ellen to make a living.

"Do you think it's something I could do if I don't go back to nursing?" She asked.

"It would be easy, and there are plenty doing it. No one checks on where women have their lying-in, no one really bothers with the way they are cared for. You have to register the births, but that is easy. If the babies die, as they often do," she fixed Amelia with a stare, before she went on, "there's the business of registering the death. You have to get a doctor; it can go to the coroner. But babies die so easy, sometimes they don't take their first breath, you must have seen that on the wards, haven't you?"

Amelia knew, some babies were born still and un-breathing, many died within a few hours of their delivery.

Ellen Dane went on to paint a picture of a different aspect of her work, a potential to help in other ways and make a tidy profit as she did so. Society frowned on women who were pregnant and unmarried and had little sympathy for the babies they brought into the world. The poor laws were completely stacked in favour of men, who did not have to support their illegitimate children. This harsh legislation had been designed to stop the number of unwanted babies being born from rising, but had not worked. In fact, even more unwanted babies were being born. But they were seen as worthless, unlovable and, worst of all, easily disposed of. Amelia had seen women in the hospital giving birth, some delighted with the babies they produced, but some clearly daunted by the prospect of having to provide for these little ones on their own. It began to make sense to her. Now Ellen began to tell her about how women often asked her to keep the babies or put them up for adoption. Sometimes they asked her to help them quietly suffocate their babies. It was best done at birth so that the death would be attributed to the child's failure to breathe – a common cause of still-birth. Dane had understood, at once, what this meant as a midwife. She knew that if a baby had never breathed at the start of its life it was easy to register the death as natural; neither the mother nor the midwife would come under any suspicion. Similarly, sometimes a mother would roll over on a sleeping baby when they shared a bed, again the coroner would accept this as an accident. Dane knew she could easily help a baby slip away in this way by the gentle pressure of a pillow on its face. She told an astonished Amelia about how she helped the desperate mothers out.

While George dozed by the fire and little Ellen slept in her cot, Ellen Dane went on to talk even more about her business. She carried on disclosing her professional secrets to her astonished friend. She explained that, in some instances, the mothers would beg her to keep the children in her home. They would pay a weekly fee or a one-off payment and Dane would keep the child in her care. She kept them in her home and looked after them. Dane had extended this part of the business by advertising her services as a nurse or offering a permanent adoption. She had been amazed at how easily and quickly this business had grown. Adoption was largely unregulated and it was easy for a well spoken, educated woman to persuade a mother to let her care for the child. This was all organised with the payment of a one-off fee, the child was handed over, and was usually never looked for by its mother again. Amelia was fascinated, listening to her friend telling her without shame or guilt of the service she was providing. She spoke of her costs and overheads; she talked of making the most of her profits. She stated without any embarrassment that the best way to make a profit from the weekly fee was to spend as little as possible on the children. What she went on to describe was neglect. Underfeeding kept the children weak and stopped them growing. When they cried or put up any kind of a fight, Dane used a range of patent medicines to quiet them, these often contained opiates and alcohol, though they were supposed to help with colic and the like. Gradually the children would waste away, overcome by the "quietness" as the opiates were often called. They would eventually die. "There's even a name for it," Dane confided in Amelia, "*marasmus*. They write that on the death certificate…and they never investigate it."

Before she left the Thomas' home Ellen sat down again with Amelia and told her that her way of making a living was easy and rewarding. She went on to explain how the weekly fee was not as lucrative as the one off payments for formal adoptions. "I know you're comfortable, now, Amelia. Cousin George will provide well for you. But if you ever have to stand on your own two feet and make your way in the world, think about my little business and how well I live on it." Amelia waved her advice away, saying that she would never need to go down that route. She flushed and Ellen thought it was her disapproval of baby farming. "I know, I know. You'd never consider…"

Amelia looked her in the eye, "No, Ellen, I don't disapprove. I've listened carefully to all you have told me. Don't think I am looking down on you, you've seen a way to make a living and get on in the world. I am safe in my life, married to George. I can raise my little family here. Go on, do what you have to do."

As Ellen left, Amelia watched her go. Her blush had not been one of moral superiority or condemnation of the woman's work. Her blush marked her delicious admiration for Ellen Dane's cleverness and the thought that she, one day, might be able to be like her.

Chapter 4: Hard Labour

1879

The whole business of the death certificates and undertakers' involvement had led Amelia to this. She hated finding herself in this position; her sentence could have been much harsher, she was lucky that her conviction was for "cruelty" rather than murder. She'd been brought to the house of correction in a horrible black carriage, windowless and dark. The humiliation of being stripped and examined, forced into a yellow shift (yellow, she was told, meant that she was a hard labour prisoner). For a woman used to changing her name, she did not find it too hard to be called by a number: the number was also on her cell door and pinned to her dress.

Her cell was small and dark, her bed a hard wooden bench – she was not allowed a mattress as part of her punishment. The place was silent most of the time, and Amelia hated silence, this was another element of the punishment regime that she had to endure. And the routine was a harsh, punitive one. Each morning she would be roused early from her cell, she was allowed to wash once a day, hands and face only; she hated the restriction as she was used to being clean and scrubbed, her nursing training had made this a habit. Once dressed, she joined the other women to do household chores, cleaning, cooking and washing clothes. Bells signalled when to eat, pray and go to work. Amelia's work was picking oakum. The tiresome chore of many prisoners and workhouse inmates involved unpicking oily ropes, reclaiming the oakum to be re-used by ship-builders. She despised the work, she despised the filthy air filled with fibre that clung to her hair and filled her lungs, and she despised the painful blisters on her hands. She did count her blessings that she was not a man;

their hard labour was working the treadmill, achingly tiring, pointless work. The women often heard their cries of pain and realised that they often injured themselves, pulling muscles and tearing tendons. Amelia took comfort in her breaks where she could read her bible and reflect on her crime. Her reflection always came to the same point, she would not be caught again and she would not end up in prison.

She'd been a baby farmer for quite some time, now. Her life with George and Ellen had been peaceful and easy. But being married to a much older man had its disadvantages. George had died when Ellen was two years old. He'd died at home, and Amelia had cared for him. He'd had some vile gastric infection, she knew from her hospital experience. She had cleaned after him and tried to get him to eat and drink. The coroner had recorded his cause of death as diarrhoea. His family had looked at her with distrust and suspicion at the funeral. George did leave money; Amelia could have lived comfortably on what he left. The marriage had not lasted long and she knew his sons thought they should have had had some of the money but she was now a widow with a small child to look after. She held her head high, looked them in the eye as if to dare them to question her new fortune. They left; she did not see them again.

It was easy to set up her property as a lying-in house. She'd used a little of her money to find someone to look after Ellen for her, settling her with a family who lived out in the country. Ellen could have a childhood like the one she'd had. Without her daughter, Amelia was able to help women deliver their babies and look after them for a while afterwards. One or two had asked her, pleaded with her, to let the little ones die. Amelia knew how to let them suffocate as they were delivered. This would raise no suspicion; infant death was so common, even the undertakers were never surprised. There was something in their faces and the colour of their skin that confirmed they had never lived to draw a breath.

She had not lost touch with Ellen Dane, though they were business rivals. Around the time of George's death when little Ellen had been sent away, Ellen Dane began to feel nervous and worried. She was aware that she had come to the attention of the police. Reputations spread easily and infant neglect was a talking point among the gossips of the town. Dane felt they were closing in on her and so she wound up her business. Amelia could only see this as an opportunity for her own business to expand. Sitting in the House of Correction now, however, she could see the sense in Dane's actions. What Ellen had done was not attractive to Amelia, herself.

Ellen Dane had taken advantage of the busy Bristol shipping lines and booked herself a passage to America. She took only a few possessions and a lot of cash. She could survive for some time on her savings and was sure there were American women and desperate immigrants who would be happy to pay for her services. The gap she had left gave Amelia the opportunity to expand her work and she moved further into the adoption business. The first precaution she had taken was the practice of adopting aliases. Her first advertisements for adoptions had been in the names of "Mrs Harding" and "Mrs Smith." Using the aliases and moving house frequently had kept her ahead of the law. She vowed, sitting here in the dark, she would never be caught like this again. Her mind worked quickly. In future, if she carried on with the business she would continue using a number of names and addresses; she would move the babies around so they were hard to trace. There were enough women who would take them in and care for them for a short while for the right price. She would also dispense with the need for undertakers and death certificates and would make her own arrangements for the babies' disposal. She bided her time. She did her hard labour.

Six months later she returned home. This was a very different home from the one she had lived in with George. By this time, she had a second husband, William Dyer. Ellen had been brought back to live with them and Amelia also had another daughter, Polly plus a little boy, Willie. She had met William through her old workmates in the corset making business, shortly after being widowed. His father was well known in corset making circles. When they married he had been working in a sugar factory; he was safe and secure and younger than her, too. It suited her way of life to have a husband. Couples preferred to give their babies for adoption when there was a mother and a father. Her new husband was a simple labouring man without education; she remembered with a little disgust that he had signed the marriage register with a cross. William had been in the house while Amelia was helping women have their babies and had known (along with the other children) about the little ones who stayed and grew weaker and died. But he did not get involved with this business. Like a lot of men, he thought childbirth and its mysteries were women's business. He had quietly accepted the deaths of two of their own children, victims of infant mortality, themselves, buried in tiny graves in the churchyard.

Amelia returned from prison looking very different. William and the children noticed that she had lost a lot of weight; her fine upright figure was much changed. She had broken fingernails and scarred hands which she kept hidden in her apron pocket. Her teeth had always given her trouble, were much worse now, blackened and painful. From the time she came home, she found it hard to sleep and often slept sitting in a chair. The children had been fine, William had worked hard to look after them and Polly had taken on the role of little mother to them all. William had been working in a vinegar factory at the time of her arrest but had lost that job. After she returned, he found work labouring, but it was low paid. Amelia realised she needed to earn again.

Amelia did, nevertheless, have to deal with a big disappointment on her return. She had been so happy to have her daughter Ellen back with her, home where she belonged. However, Ellen, who had seen and been involved in Amelia's work and had witnessed the child cruelty that took her mother away from them, left. Somehow, Amelia had hoped they would stay a family. She had always thought that Ellen would remain with her as she grew older. She didn't realise that farming Ellen out all those years ago had broken the bonds between mother and child. She was fifteen, now, old enough to understand what was going on in their home, Ellen did not like it. She had spent a lot of her young life with another family, so leaving was easy. No one, at the time, knew where she had gone or how she supported herself. Many years later, Polly thought she heard Ellen had married and settled. It suited them all to believe that.

Home from prison, seeing the family struggle, Amelia had to decide what to do next. She was clear that, if she was going to continue her baby-farming, things would have to change. However, William's father saw their sorry state and came to them with an offer of help. He knew Amelia had been in the corset-making industry when she was younger. He helped her find a place in one of the factories. Polly and Willie were sent to school, living a normal life for a change and for six months watched their mother setting off for work each day.

Chapter 5: Evelina's Story

March 1896

Evelina looked at the paper again and felt the ache in her breasts - the sting of milk coming in - at the thought of giving up her baby. Tightness gripped her, with the realisation that she'd lose her golden haired girl; a gasp of sadness escaped her throat. She'd known from the start of her pregnancy that she'd have to find some solution to this difficult problem; she'd have to look for a different way of life.

It seemed like some kind of godsend. She'd placed her advert in the *Bristol Times and Mirror*. It had been direct and to the point: "Wanted, respectable woman to take young child." It was clear, simple and cost very little. When the paper came out, she'd hurried to buy her copy to see her notice in print. Now, here, next to her own she could see the solution to her problem. The address was in Reading, far away for sure, but near enough to visit Doris, if she saved her train fares carefully. The words danced before her eyes but she read them again to make sure she was clear about the message: *"Married couple with no family would adopt healthy child, nice country home. Terms - £10."*

Walking back to Amy's rooms, the place she called home for now, the rain soaked through her thin coat, she shivered and quickened her pace. She gripped the bag containing the precious gift she'd shopped for. She hadn't been able to resist them when she saw them in the shoe-maker's window; she'd parted with her money without a thought. The boots were tooled, fine leather-work and even stitching; buttons set like little soldiers in a neat parade-ground row. She'd pictured Doris in them, taking her first steps – clip-clopping on the paved street and laughing with delight. Then, she realised she'd not be there to see the transformation from baby to little girl. The thought upset her but she put it to the back of her mind.

This advertisement held the answer to her problems; an older couple, respectable and settled. They sounded suitable. She tested the name out, Harding... it sounded safe, reliable and secure. Mr and Mrs Harding - she pictured them holding hands standing by a fireplace in a comfortable home. They might well be the ones to give Doris the start in life she needed. They'd feed and clothe her, teach her manners and help her out into the world. She began to daydream that her little girl would be sent to school, wear pretty things, read, write, embroider and play the piano... She shook herself back to reality. Doris's needs were more basic and more urgent: food on the table, a home with some degree of love in it and no shame of being the bastard child of a barmaid. Evelina hoped they'd keep in touch, let her visit and write letters, maybe she'd even see Doris in those boots.

There was no way that Mr Wells was going to let her back to work in the Plough Hotel with a child to look after; for a start she'd got the "fallen woman" stigma to overcome and there was no wet nurse or relative to take the baby when she did the long shifts behind the bar. As the landlord of the hotel, he knew the reputation of barmaids; the jobs were often taken up by women with questionable histories. But Evelina was not like them, she'd come to Cheltenham to work, away from the small town life of her country home. She'd decided, long ago, that she'd rather the fashionable town than the life of a farmer's wife. She was pretty, blonde and had a good figure. She was witty and humorous. He liked her working in the hotel. Mr Wells had been more understanding than many bosses would have been. There were many like her who had to put themselves at the mercy of the parish and take their little ones to the workhouse or worse, like Amy had, dump the little bundle on the steps at the convent door.

Evelina had been shocked when she'd heard her friend Amy's story. She'd hidden her pregnant state from everyone. She'd had her baby in secret and searched, without success, for someone to take the child. What must it have been like for that desperate young woman? And where was the father? He'd have been safe in his respectable family home somewhere, not giving a thought to the girl he'd ruined. Amy had gone to the orphanage in her home town and asked at the door whether they'd take the child. The response had been cold, chilling and heartless. Her child had been conceived in sin, marked by sin, would taint the other orphans with its sinfulness and mark them for the fires of Hell, where she was bound for sure.

Amy had abandoned her baby boy, hoping he'd be raised as a foundling. Next day she'd packed her things and moved to Cheltenham. Making a new life for herself, she'd found work at the pub where she and Evelina had become friends.

For now, Evelina had been staying with Amy, but would return to her rooms with Mrs Pockett, the landlady who had helped her get the barmaid job in the hotel in the first place. Martha Pockett was an older woman, kind and helpful. She had never judged Evelina for her pregnancy or for bringing little Doris into the world. The rooms were always there for her - rooms where, Evelina swore, no man would be welcomed to get her into this state again. Theirs was a good relationship, Evelina looked after the old, infirm woman as well as lodging with her. She'd not asked her to leave when the child was born, but Evelina had had a few thoughts about the strain on the older woman of having a young baby in the house. Evelina had the option of returning to her family home, they would have taken her in but it was a small town community with small town attitudes and she'd have been marked as a fallen woman and prayed over in the church. No, she could not return to that, her best chance was to have Doris adopted then return to her old job and her old life.

Evelina had a choice to make for herself and her lovely Doris. She could only stay with Amy for a few more days; she really had to start to support herself again. Through her tears, she looked again at the paper. This was a chance for Evelina to get her life back, the solution she had been searching for. The rain left off a bit. Her pace quickened. There was a way forward. She'd answer the advert and secure a future for her precious little girl.

Chapter 6: The meeting

March 1896

When she arrived back at Amy's, Evelina warmed herself by the fire. Her thin, white hands were shaking from the walk home and from the fear of what she was about to do. Doris, angelic and rosy was sleeping in a little box, watched by Amy's landlady's nine year old daughter, Nancy. Evelina gave her a penny and she ran off happily.

She found paper and ink. Then, sitting at the table, began her letter. She asked the Hardings if they could give her precious child a home. She felt the shame of her unmarried state and did not want Doris to live under the stigma of illegitimacy, so she signed her letter as if she were a widow. The name she picked was Mrs Scott. When she had finished the letter, she read it and re-read it. It had to be just right. It seemed ridiculous to her that she was trying to make the right impression on these strangers. It was they who should be assuring her of their kindness and respectability. Anyone anywhere could adopt or give a child for adoption, so much depended on trust. The law did not safeguard the babies or the mothers. There were agreements drawn up by notaries and deals were struck, but the law did not provide proper protection if things went wrong. Evelina knew she had to stand her ground if she was to see Doris again.

By the time the letter was finished, Doris was stirring, ready to be fed. Evelina put the kettle on the fire and began to make tea for Amy when she came in from work. The letter could go first thing in the morning; meanwhile she'd nurse her child and hold her close this evening.

A few days later she received a reply from Oxford Road, Reading. Mrs Harding wrote: "I should be glad to have a dear little baby girl, one I could bring up and call my own. We are plain, homely people, in fairly good circumstances. I don't want a child for money's sake, but for company and home comfort ... Myself and my husband are dearly fond of children. I have no child of my own. A child with me will have a good home and a mother's love."

Reading and re-reading the letter, Evelina was assured this was the right thing to do. She thrust it under Amy's gaze many times to check she agreed. Amy almost laughed as she handed it back, "I've told you enough times. It sounds good! She's able to read and write well, so must be educated and refined. She'll be a good mother to Doris! Go on Evelina, take this chance to get your life back. Doris will be in good hands. You'll be able to go back to work, move back to your old digs and everything in the garden will be rosy!"

Her next obstacle was to find the £10 fee. It was a huge sum and it would take a barmaid a long time to save that much. She had asked the Hardings if they'd accept a more affordable weekly fee but Mrs Harding was adamant and wanted the payment in advance. She had no choice but to agree to pay the sum required.

They continued to write, making arrangements about the meeting - the handover. Evelina was happy that Mrs Harding wrote about future visits to see the child growing up, their commitment to the Church of England and how delightful it would be to have Doris growing up in the countryside. Evelina was pleased to think her baby might be far from the danger of catching small-pox growing up in the fresh air. As they made plans for the meeting where Doris would be given to her new parents, she also learned that Mrs Harding was going to visit a sick friend (surely the woman was good through and through) and would bring a warm shawl for the baby, in case the day was cold. Evelina was growing more and more convinced that she was making the right choice.

She had most of the ten pounds saved. Although she had not been working, she only had to pay a little rent. She could not go to the baby's father; he'd made it clear this was her problem from the start. His coaxing looks and gentle words had dried up very quickly once he'd got what he wanted. He had given her some money at the time she found herself in trouble and she'd put it away for Doris. She could use that. He'd also given her one or two pieces of jewellery when he'd been trying to win her affections, she was sure they weren't worth a lot; they could go the pawn shop. She thought about taking the beautiful little boots back but couldn't find the heart to do it. Mr Wells would give her an advance on her wages, he'd help her out. He knew the man who'd fathered the child was too influential to upset; any scandal could be detrimental to the pub and its respectable reputation. She arranged to meet the Hardings and went to work getting the money together.

By the time of the meeting, she had her money and a little cardboard box of things for Doris. Along with the leather boots, she'd packed clothes and napkins. She'd taken Doris to have her vaccination against small pox - who knew what kinds of people she might mix with in the future, what kind of germs were out there? She slipped the vaccination certificate into the box with the other items. She dressed her child in a fawn coloured outfit, a little jacket with a shawl knitted into it.

Her poor, young face showed the sadness this was causing her. Amy had washed her face with a rough cloth and helped her comb her hair. She kept telling Evelina she was doing the right thing. Doris could only benefit from this, her life could be so much better with a respectable family, in a respectable home. She reminded her of the dirty urchins they saw in the streets, hungry and without protection from all kinds of danger. Doris would be spared all that, she told her, Doris would have a good life. Evelina knew the sense of what she was saying; she held her tears back and put on a brave face. She prepared to meet the Hardings.

The meeting took place in Martha Pockett's house where Evelina was living once again. It was a cold morning, so the precaution about warm clothes for the child made sense. Evelina was surprised to find that Mrs Harding, who was in fact Amelia Dyer, was older than she'd expected her to be. She had thought she'd be handing her child to a young woman with the energy to raise her as her own. However, she could not doubt the woman's gentleness when she looked after Doris, making sure her head was warm in the chill wind. There was no sign of Mr Harding. He had, however, apparently drawn up a paper – an agreement of adoption – which stated that his wife would be the carer for the child. The paper was dated, thirty-first of March, the year of one thousand eight hundred and ninety six. There was a place for Martha Pockett to witness the agreement, at her home address: 23 Manchester Street, Cheltenham. It all seemed so plausible, so real and properly undertaken. Evelina was relieved that the woman was affectionate towards Doris, so she handed over her daughter, a cardboard box of clothes and the £10 fee.

Then the time came for them to leave, Evelina's heart was breaking. But she did not cry but stayed calm and positive. However, as Mrs Harding left for the station, Evelina grabbed her own coat and bonnet and said she'd go with them. Mrs Harding had not expected this, but welcomed her along, fussing over the child all the time and chatting to ease the atmosphere.

They reached the station. Mrs Harding went to collect a big, old carpet bag from the cloakroom. She told Evelina it contained some eggs and clothes she was passing on to a friend. But she looked awkward, there, with the shabby bag, the cardboard box of clothes and the little baby wrapped in a shawl. Evelina realised that the woman had to change trains at Gloucester, to catch her train to Reading. She decided to go along with her for part of the journey; it would be easier for Doris and would give her just a short while more with the baby she loved so much. Harding seemed totally at ease with her travelling with them, still chatting and making a fuss of the baby, referring to her as "my dear little girl."

At Gloucester, Mrs Harding bundled the child, along with all her other belongings, onto the 5.20 to Reading. It would be very cold and dark by the time they reached their destination, by which time Evelina would be in Cheltenham. Evelina strained to catch a last glimpse of the little child as the train pulled noisily and smokily away from the platform. She watched it until it was out of sight.

Evelina returned to Cheltenham a sad and broken woman. All she could do was wait, patiently, for the letters promised by Mrs Harding about the child's progress. A letter soon arrived and, to her surprise, Evelina saw it had been written from a London address. Harding told her that she'd had to go to London because her sister was ill, she reassured Evelina that the child had travelled well. She promised to write again. She never did.

Chapter 7: Jane Smith

January 1896

Jane Smith was very troubled. There were too many questions she could not ask and could not find any answers to. She wished she had never left the workhouse. In fact that was her first question, why had she left? If she had done things differently, she would not be where she was now. Safe and warm, she'd be wrapped in routine and not worrying every moment of every day.

Jane had been in the workhouse for two years; she had not been happy or unhappy. Workhouse life was tidy and ordered, from the bell that called them to morning prayers to the silent, dark dormitory where she slept with seven other women. She remembered the comfort of hearing them breathe, the rhythms of their soft snores and mutterings. She remembered the comfort of the well-washed striped-cotton dress and the white bonnet which marked the older women as suitable for certain chores. She did the same kind of work she had done as a wife, the same kind of work she was doing now. The older women worked in the garden, not digging like the fit young ones, but weeding, picking and tending to the vegetables. They cooked the meals for the inmates of the workhouse and washed their dishes and clothes. They sat in their caps and shawls sewing shirts for the men and mending the well-worn dresses of the women and children. They also helped with cleaning the children and tending to the sore, calloused hands of the women who spent their days picking oakum. She had known her place and had done her work.

Things were so different now. She didn't really know what she was doing in Caversham. Her work was looking after the house, the children and the babies. Little sickly ones they were. Their weak state brought to her mind the way she had lost her own three children. They had seemed healthy and strong at birth but, one by one, they had developed the pale skin and raspy coughs of the consumptive. It was not right for a woman to lose all her children like that. Jane and William had done their best and had looked for help where they could get it. But the wages of a cleaner and a labourer could not pay a doctor's bills, and so could not snatch the children from the death that their poverty ensured. She'd gone on with life, mourned their loss. She'd become a valued member of staff in the solicitor's firm where she had cleaned up after the lawyers and clerks. At least she had still had William.

There was another question to dwell on. Had she done right by William? She'd left her home in Swansea to be with him, this bright, strong man from Bristol who had swept her off her feet. She'd never left her home-town before, so the move to a new city had brought excitement to her life and she had taken to it well. They were simple folk, never likely to be rich, but happy to work hard and make a home. They had rented a house in Bristol, brought their children into the world and had buried them one by one. They had very little money and no savings to speak of. When the bills came in, they struggled to meet them. But they got by. When Jane was sixty-eight, her William had died. She had paid the bill for his funeral and sent him off in a plank coffin to the graveyard where he was laid under a little wooden cross. She'd invited the mourners back to her house and served them ale and pork pies. She had given him a good send off. Yes, she'd done right by him. But then, like so many women of her time, she had struggled to pay the rent. The landlord had given her no leeway and there were other bills to pay. So she found herself homeless and had made her way to the workhouse.

She looked into the window of this little shop front in Oxford Road. There were words on signs and she knew some of the letters, they were about children. There were pictures of sad, neglected little waifs and she thought of her own babies and then of the babies in her care. What was this place? This was her next question. Jane was curious, she seemed rooted to the spot. Her eyes were brimming with tears.

She thought of the house she lived in, babies and children were always coming and going. Women in a certain condition, as they said, arrived, stayed a few days, a week or so, sometimes more. She knew Amelia helped to deliver them and cared for their babies in the first weeks of their lives. There were always bloodied sheets and rags to wash, childbirth was a messy business. She, herself, looked after the children Willie, Alfred, Lily and Annie. She cooked their meals, cleaned up after them, and washed their clothes. That all made sense.

What she could not understand as she tried to make sense of it all, were the comings and goings of little ones into and out of the house. Amelia, her friend, her adopted "sister," dealt with the babies, brought them in, let them sleep, got her daughter Polly or Jane to feed and quieten them. But they were fed with water mixed with cornflour, which was not enough to feed a hungry baby. They were also given powders to help them sleep, to take them into "quietness." She had asked where they went when the babies left and was so confused by some of the answers she had been given. They were moved to London or Reading to live with other mothers; they were sickly and taken back to their mothers; they were in the workhouse or the orphanage because "Mother," Amelia, could not help them. Jane liked to believe these stories, it was easier that way. If she started to think about what could be the real story she became upset. She did her chores and looked after the children as well as she could.

Another question that rattled in her head, but she did not want to answer it, was why Polly and the others said that Mother's job was "angel maker"? She pushed that one from her mind. If it popped up she pictured Amelia as an angel herself, like the picture there had been in the workhouse of a guardian angel, in long robes with wings from its shoulder to the floor, guiding little children along a country path. And if Amelia was a nurse as she said she was, she had never had a reason to question her ways, why didn't she make the babies better?

And here was a question. Why was Jane called "Granny"? She'd never raised her children to see them grown with children of their own. It was strange to have this name, now. Though she was happy to be called that by Willie and his sisters; it sounded strange when Polly and Amelia called her that – they were grown women themselves. But Amelia was called "Mother" by so many that knew her, Jane supposed it made some kind of sense.

Then there was Amelia herself. Why did she have so many different names? Ann or Annie, Smith, Thomas, Dyer, Harding, Stansfield, Weymouth…? Jane knew she was really Amelia Dyer and had been married to a Mr Thomas before his death. But Jane had always been Jane, plain Jane and the only name she wanted was her husband's - Smith. Jane Smith, plain and simple. Changing names was all part of the moving from place to place routine Amelia followed, the strange knockings on the door from time to time and of people asking where their children were. But Jane knew that Amelia could come up with an answer to any question posed. She was quick thinking. And it the knocking on the door became too insistent, she swiftly packed up and moved them all on again.

Why? This was a question Jane asked herself many, many times. For a start, why had Amelia befriended her and brought her with her when she left the workhouse? She remembered the first time she'd seen her, when she'd joined the women in the dreary dormitory. The new inmate had been striking to look at, tall and dignified in the way she'd held herself. Her eyes had fixed everyone with their stare. This had annoyed the pauper attendants who ran the place but she hadn't been intimidated by them. Where the workhouse women were cowed and looked defeated, Amelia had stood tall and defied the whole institution. She was there because she was impoverished, not defeated. She would leave when she could and return to her family. It was just a passing problem. The truth was that she had been in an asylum, where she had been treated for insanity. Now apparently cured, she'd been in the infirmary before she'd moved into the care of the parish, where she was declared ready for work. Jane had little understanding of madness; to her Amelia Dyer was not mad.

Amelia, however, had made no secret of her mental state; it was almost as if she had wanted people to know about it. Maybe she used it as insurance against a time when she might be locked up again, and everyone would remember that she had been like this before. She struck up a friendship with Jane and the two began to chat and confide in one another. Amelia told Jane of her time in the asylum and about how she sometimes became so distressed that she thought about killing herself. Jane was shocked, everyone knew taking your own life was a terrible sin, bound to send you off to the fires of Hell for all eternity. Jane thought she would see her days out in Barton Regis Workhouse but Amelia talked of getting her life back together when she was ready and of taking her children with her when she went. Jane was surprised to hear that Amelia's children were in the workhouse, too. There had been four children, Jane now knew three of them - Alfred, Lily, Annie and a baby but she never knew her name. Amelia told her these were all adopted children; Jane admired and respected her big heart and her kindness. However, the baby girl did not leave the workhouse with them. She disappeared but Amelia never mourned her loss. Jane thought this odd because she still thought with sadness of her own little ones. Jane was also amazed that the other children never asked about their "sister." Now, all this time later she was not so surprised. They saw so many babies come and go it was probably easier for them not to become attached. Someone had told Jane that the little child lost in the workhouse had, in fact, been sent off to Canada by the workhouse Guardians; she hoped the baby had a good life there.

Amelia had sometimes been allowed to supervise in the children's section of the workhouse, where she would watch them doing their work and learning their lessons. Not many of the women in the workhouse had been as educated as Amelia, so she helped the children with their reading and writing. They practiced writing verses from the Bible like "Suffer little children to come unto me" and guidelines for life like "Be true in Heart" or "Neither a borrower nor a lender be." Jane recognised some of these sayings, even though her own reading and writing were poor.

Now Jane questioned herself again, why had she let Amelia talk her into leaving with them when she and her children left the workhouse? At the time, she'd felt as if she had been picked for some special kind of friendship, promised a new and better life. And it had all happened quickly so that Jane had not had the time it usually took her to think over such a big decision. When they got out of the workhouse, Amelia had said that Jane could be her special helper and could come and live with them all and look after the children as if they were her own grandchildren. She would take her away from the drudgery of the workhouse, with its rules and routines. She would even pay her to be a kind of housekeeper. A shilling a week was the promised amount. Now, Jane, standing in this Caversham road, was feeling the despair of her dependence on Amelia Dyer and wondered why she had never been paid that shilling a week. She saw money coming into the house and bank-notes tucked into Mother's big apron pocket. There must have been plenty but she never saw any of it and that little wage would have given her some freedom, some opportunity. Here she was, totally dependent on the woman who had freed her from the workhouse and confused, so very confused.

She remembered the days leading up to leaving the workhouse well. Suddenly, out of the blue, one morning Amelia Dyer had asked for permission to leave for a day to visit her grown-up daughter. She told Jane afterwards that she had gone to get the money she needed to leave. In a matter of hours she had secured not just the money, but a place to live and the freedom of three of her children too. She'd then approached Jane, telling her: "We are going tomorrow. Start getting your things together." Jane had few things, just the clothes she had come in with, her prayer book and some personal papers. Jane did not have time to stop and think. Amelia blustered and took over, like a whirlwind. Jane tried to explain her hesitation and was put down with, "Nonsense, Jane, you shall come with me. I'll keep you and pay you a wage. We'll be the best of friends, like sisters, and you'll be out of this place for good." Jane went along with her. The next day they had left, with the three children and Jane had started her new life as "Granny Smith."

And what had happened from that day onwards had made Jane's life busy, confusing and emotional. How Amelia and the children coped with the comings and goings of women and babies was a mystery to her. She liked to hold the little ones and feel their fast pulses racing, feel them squeezing her finger in their little fists and see how they guzzled the watery food that was offered. But one by one their pulses slowed, their grips weakened and their eating ceased. In order to block out this horror, Jane would throw herself into her work scrubbing the floors, boiling sheets and cooking the meals. She took little pride in these jobs, especially as they might move at any moment into the next rented property. However she grew fond of the children Amelia called her own, Annie, Alfred, Willie and Lily. They helped her make sense of the world. They could not answer her questions, though because they took life with Amelia as normal and accepted Mother's word on everything. Polly and her husband Arthur Palmer were something different. Jane never took to him, she thought him vain and snobbish. She disliked his indolence, sitting by the fire in Dyer's house, while others did all the work. He expected Jane to wait on him as if he were the master of the house. When Polly was there, Jane took second place as Mother's principal helper, although Polly's jobs were different from Jane's. She'd watch from her quiet seat in the corner, as Polly sorted through bags of baby clothes, some of them were for the pawn shop and some were kept for the babies in the house. Polly also kept an eye on the babies when Amelia went off on trips, some days leaving with a baby wrapped in a shawl, returning empty-handed. Other days Amelia would go to collect a baby, returning from some distant town with an infant to care for and a pocket stuffed with paper money. On a few occasions, Jane was distressed to see Amelia leave with a parcel, a bundle in her hands or in her bag, and Jane wanted to ask what she was carrying, but did not dare. Where did the babies go? Were they ever coming back?

Polly also ran errands for her mother, dropping letters and parcels to the post. Jane did not know what these were, but she saw that Amelia would spend long periods of time at the table, writing letters in her small, neat hand. These were the letters to newspapers seeking prospective adoptions. Jane could see the kind of letters and documents they were, even if she could not decipher the written words. Polly was also the one sent to the apothecary for Amelia's medicine. Jane knew enough, in fact had known in the old workhouse days, of Amelia's terrible teeth and the pain they gave her. Jane wondered why she had not had them pulled. In the Bristol streets where Jane had lived, there was a barber who would pull teeth for poor, tooth-ache sufferers. In the workhouse, someone from the infirmary could have done it. But Amelia never sought help, she relied on pain relief. Jane knew this came in the form of a liquid she carried in her apron pocket. It must have been laudanum, lots of people took it to relieve their various agonies, but Jane did not ask. She watched, though, and saw how it would affect her moods. On these trips for medicine, Polly often returned with pills and powders for the babies too. Jane knew some were for colic or diarrhoea. She also knew the babies were given the laudanum as well, she'd heard it spoken of by others, mothers and child-minders alike as it made babies quiet and stopped their appetites. Jane watched, distressed but unable to act against or question Amelia.

There were other questions she could find no answers to. She wondered about the smell of stale air and rot that overwhelmed the household sometimes. One day, she and Willie had gone from room to room seeking the source of the smell. They'd tracked if down to a locked, metal trunk in Amelia's bedroom. They mentioned the smell to Amelia, who'd said she thought there was a dead rat under the floorboards. A few days later, Jane saw the trunk left open, it was empty and the smell subsided.

Jane wondered why the police called to the door from time to time. They were never invited in, and Amelia usually answered their questions on the doorstep. Sometimes they would move soon after the police had called. Jane wanted to shout "Why?" She desperately wanted to say "Answer me, please, put my mind at rest." But did not, she just went from day to day.

The shop door opened and Jane was brought back to the moment, here, in Oxford Road. A woman with a kind face and soft voice was asking her if she was all right. Everything about this woman seemed the opposite of Amelia Dyer – where Dyer was tall, this woman was small; where Dyer looked sternly at Jane, this woman's eyes showed concern and empathy; where Dyer carried herself tall and upright, this woman's movements were fluid and gentle. The woman took Jane's hands and led her inside. The shop front led to a room which was neat and orderly. There were chairs and a table that was covered with a crisp, white cloth. The room was fresh and clean and Jane recognised the smell of the wax polish she had been accustomed to using on the workhouse panels and banisters. Jane felt a comfort she had not felt for a long time. The woman found Jane a seat and poured her a cup of tea. Jane asked where she was. The woman told Jane she was Mrs Bennett and that her husband was an officer of a new organisation devoted to the care of children called: the NSPCC. Jane had never heard of it. While Mrs Bennett explained about the work they did, Jane let her tears fall. She told Mrs Bennett about the life she lived with the Dyer family. She explained that Amelia adopted children and supposedly cared for them. She told the woman of her confusion about the comings and goings in the house and the way that the family lived. She told her how she had never been paid. She even said she'd like to go back to the workhouse.

But then she calmed herself and regained her composure. She said she'd better be off then, she was expected at home with food for the dinner and she thanked the woman for her kindness. Leaving that place, she thought she would be able to cope better; she had cried and had expressed some of the confusion that had been overwhelming her. She set off to finish her errands and go home. She felt lighter, relieved of her burden.

What Jane had not thought about, indeed it had never crossed her mind, was that Mrs Bennett would tell her husband about her visit. He checked his documents and had no record of anyone making legal adoptions from the address in Kensington Road that Jane had given to his wife. She almost had a fit when he knocked at the door of someone he thought was Mrs Thomas a few nights later and she cursed herself and questioned her own judgement. But Mr Bennett didn't look at Jane and did not speak to her or refer to her visit. Jane sat, invisible as ever, in her seat by the fire. Mr Bennett looked around and commented that the house was fairly sparely furnished and plain. There was evidence of babies and babies' cradles and clothes. He questioned "Mrs Thomas" about the non-attendance of one of the children at school; she was humble and promised to comply in future. He inquired about adopted children and Amelia Dyer explained she often placed them with other mothers in good homes. However, he was concerned about the health of one child and pressed the women to tell him where the child came from and was given a name. When he left, he wrote to the man whose name he had been given as the child's uncle, this man later tried to contact Mrs Thomas, without success.

Mr Bennett stated, clearly and firmly, as he left, that in future Mrs Thomas should register herself as an adoptive parent and should expect to see him visiting again. She was happy with that and bade him goodbye.

When he had gone, she turned to Jane and said "Start packing, Granny! We'll be moving quite soon."

Chapter 8: Arthur Palmer

April 1896

The crowds outside Reading Courthouse waited to catch a glimpse of the monsters they'd been hearing about. It was warm for April and the onlookers were hot. The stench of sour perspiration was in the air, many of these people had been working in the heat that day before rushing to see the fiend arrive. When the cab drew up, it had trouble pulling over to take the occupants into court. Two men came out of the cab: a prison officer, looking serious in his dark uniform. Beside him, handcuffed, was Arthur Palmer, Amelia Dyer's son-in-law. The sweaty mob jeered and called out insults to the man. He did not react at all. He looked aloof and superior to the angry onlookers. Everyone noticed his outfit; he wore a long, tailored frock coat and a silk top hat, looking as though he was off to the opera, not to his own trial.

While the crowd awaited the arrival of Dyer, Arthur Palmer was taken into the courthouse. Once inside, he walked calmly. In contrast, when Amelia Dyer arrived, her step was heavy, she stumbled as she walked. He watched her coming through the courtroom door. When she saw him, she mumbled, wondering what he was doing there; otherwise she gave little away.

Arthur was first in the dock, holding his silk topper under his arm. To all in the courtroom, he looked calm and nonchalant. He was very well groomed, with his neat hair and trimmed whiskers. He'd carefully chosen a tie to go with his outfit. The charges were read: while Dyer was accused of "feloniously" killing a female child unknown; Palmer was charged with being an accessory, helping Dyer to conceal the child and escape justice. However, because they had not identified the body of the little girl that had

46

been found in the canal and the police were now finding more bodies, the case was adjourned for a week. Arthur Palmer and his mother-in-law were taken back to their cells.

Although he was not that good looking, Arthur wanted to be noticed, turn heads and have women admire him. He'd always been concerned about his appearance, carefully choosing his clothes and adopting his own style. With his perfect grooming and eye-catching clothes, he appeared to be a dashing young man about town and wealthier than he really was. Compared to his stylish, thoughtful effort with his appearance, the other men of the town looked like Neanderthals: greasy hair scraped across their pale scalps, cheap clothes with rough, hairy textures and wearing clogs or hob-nailed boots, the mark of their working-class poverty.

Arthur was different; he came from a better class. The son of a printer, he had been born in Dorset into a comfortable home. His father had died when he was quite young and his mother brought Arthur and his brother up alone, paying attention to them and fussing over their needs. She was a seamstress and dressmaker able to support her boys and see them well turned out. Arthur had never lost his sense of pride in his appearance.

At the age of sixteen, Arthur had been brave and adventurous. Without telling his mother, he travelled to Liverpool where he boarded a ship bound for New York. He told everyone he was a labourer and went off to earn his fortune. He was a good worker, full of drive and wanting success. Travel gave him a different view of the world; among other things he had developed his own style and sense of fashion. By the time he arrived back in England with savings of several hundred pounds, he was ready to start his own business.

He opened a little shop in Totterdown, on the same road as the Dyer family, Wells Road. His shop was a haberdashery or "fancy" store as it was called then. He sold ribbons and feathers, lace, buttons and bows… all the things women would use to finish their dresses and adorn their costumes. Arthur loved the way women came in to be flattered and flirt with him. He even offered them favours of a different kind and some would accept his advances. One of the customers who appeared to like him a lot was Polly Dyer. Polly liked to dress smartly and tried to look stylish when she could. She'd wear a little bonnet at a jaunty angle or a fashionable cape over her hardwearing dress. She enjoyed the little fripperies sold in Arthur's shop. He came to realise her life must be quite hard with her mother and the other children to care for, so admired her spirit and her cheerful chatty ways. He saw in her a simple, but worldly air of someone who had seen things and lived a life. Among the prudish women of the day, she stood out as someone who did not fear the body or its functions. She didn't brush his hand away if it lingered on her waist, she did not blush when he teased her by asking for a kiss.

They began to walk out together. Polly thought her mother would object. She knew the forced secrecy of their family life had produced a strain between her parents in their uncomfortable marriage. Amelia had remarried after Thomas' death, but the man she had chosen was very different from her first husband. When Polly started seeing Arthur, her mother was happy that he was a man with capital and substance. Her own husband was a working man, employed in the vinegar factory - smelling of vinegar and with rough calloused hands - his income was low because he was unskilled; it was partly because of his low income that she had had to work running her house of confinement. There was little love between Amelia and her husband. She had no problem with Polly finding some comfort and companionship with Arthur.

In due course, Arthur talked to Polly about their future and asked if she'd be his wife. She was thrilled. Polly's life was not easy and this could give her an escape route from her mother's business, her mood swings and the constant moving from place to place that had been a feature of her childhood. As they made their plans for married life, it seemed that Amelia and her husband were at the end of theirs, she was pushing him further away from the life of her family, straining an already strained relationship. Polly mentioned to her mother that Arthur would be soon approaching her step-father to discuss marriage. But Amelia was adamant that he should not speak to him but to her. Arthur, quiet and gentle in his approach, came and spoke to her. He made no secret of the fact that he was confused not to be doing the conventional thing and asking for Polly's hand from her father. He asked his prospective mother-in-law why her husband had not been part of the conversation. Amelia was cold and hard when she told him, clearly, it was nothing to do with him and he would have nothing to say on the matter. The young man put it from his mind, he'd been brought up without a father, so could accept Polly's matriarchal home.

Arthur gained an insight into the life of the family, he watched and said little. He worked out the relationships between Amelia and her children. Polly he knew was her daughter; she told him of her natural sister Ellen who had left home and not been heard of since. The others were all adopted, all different, all loyal to their "mother," Willie, who was almost grown now and the younger children Alfred, Annie and Lily. Arthur began to understand what was going on to some degree. In the time they were engaged, he saw seven different women come into Polly's house, stay for their confinement and a short while afterwards, leave without their babies. The babies were not around for long and seemed to disappear without a trace. Arthur also noticed that Polly's mother was moody and could swing from pleasant to melancholic very easily. Polly's account of her use of the medicinal drops she used to ease her pain made sense to him but he did not comment or judge. He watched and took it all in.

Close to Christmas, Polly confided that a couple had arrived on the doorstep looking for their child who had been adopted. Polly recognised them; they had come to the house before. Her mother could not give their child back because she'd given it to someone else to adopt. This woman and her husband, a governess who'd had her child out of wedlock and later married the father, had managed to track the Dyers down despite their many moves. Whatever Amelia said to them to put them off on this occasion, gave her a little space.

When Amelia took up her basket and bonnet and left the house, Arthur learned from Polly that she'd gone off for her medicine. She came back with a double dose. Arthur knew the visit of the young couple must have really upset her. He took pains to explain to his young fiancée that these were not harmless tooth-ache drops, made of oil of cloves or similar.

"You know she's taking opium?" he'd asked.

It was public knowledge that many people did, from the loftiest poet to the lowly labourer. Arthur was not a prudish man; but he began to wonder about the odd behaviour he'd seen in the Dyers' household, the angry outbursts and cruel blows. He knew Amelia hit his sweetheart and had seen her bruised and cowed by this violence.

"It's laudanum," Polly quietly admitted, "it kills her pain."

She did not tell her fiancé how many times she'd been asked to run and fetch a bottle from an apothecary, wrapped in brown paper, hidden instantly in her mother's deep apron pocket.

Amelia grew worse. A doctor was called and when he could not get sense out of her he called in a colleague. Arthur Palmer was astonished when she took up the poker to threaten the doctor. Her ramblings continued among threats to break the doctors' skulls. She told them that voices were telling her what to do, that birds and insects were driving her to this, making her mad. She repeated the phrase: "a little girl should not have to deal with this kind of thing" over and over again. Then she threatened to take her own life. Arthur watched his mother-in-law being taken off to the asylum. Maybe alarm bells started to ring then, but Arthur was not put off; he could see the potential comfort of living with the kind of income Amelia must have. He'd seen sums of money in the house, in Amelia's hands and some thrust into her deep pockets before it could be registered by the others. He wondered why they lived such meagre lives; he'd have no trouble spending that on lovely clothes for his wife and trips to the races and the sea. He was more than fond of Polly and really wanted to make a life with her. He could see that he could be part of this life, making money from the work of Amelia and Polly, money in his pocket to provide the finer things in life. Maybe he could even leave the little shop and work with them in some way or another. He was ready to become part of this seedy world and that was how he found himself in court in 1896.

When Amelia came back from the asylum she looked well and healthy. She'd put on weight, was more cheerful and her moods were not so frightening. Arthur thought she was well again. He did not realise the strain she was under, living in fear of being visited again by the couple looking for their child. He was surprised by what she did next and curious as to why Polly stayed with her in her chaotic life. First, Amelia left her husband and took all five children in her care with her. One of these "children" was Polly, even though she was twenty two by now. Her mother kept her close and seemed able to control her. They moved from place to place, giving him different addresses round Bristol, turning up in different houses on different streets. Polly never, however, lost touch with her fiancé.

Arthur approached her again, saying he wanted to go ahead with the wedding. He needed some details to have the banns put up. She put him off. And while he waited, things changed quite a lot at home. Amelia was worried about being left alone when Polly left the family and when

51

Willie went off to join the navy. She began to sink once more, Arthur saw her spirits drop. However it was the reappearance of the couple on the doorstep, this time with a constable in tow that set her off into her next bout of illness. Arthur never understood why she was not arrested but she went back to the asylum of her own accord. The people at the asylum mentioned that she'd tried to drown herself by throwing herself into a puddle, all she had done was merely managed to soak her skirts. This did not surprise Arthur Palmer, who was becoming used to her public displays and dramatic performances. However, she was admitted and stayed calm. Two weeks later she was released and Arthur and Polly went ahead with their wedding.

By now, Arthur was so sure he wanted to make a life with Polly that he spent a large amount of his savings on furniture for their home. He had let his business go and had a new job as a travelling salesman. And Amelia returned to her husband. All should have been well. Polly was happy to be married, for the first time in her life she was free from her mother's influence. The proud young couple moved into their well furnished home, comfortable and secure.

That should have been it for Arthur. He should have done well for himself and his wife. They were happy, they were in love and they had managed to move away from the domineering Amelia Dyer. Things were looking rosy. Polly was a worldly little woman; there was not much she had not seen. She was compliant and willing to please him. She was not like the other girls of her time, she was open and relaxed when they made love and he enjoyed the way she wriggled and moaned under him. Polly seemed to grow into her new role as his wife, with a confident air and was more relaxed than he'd ever seen her.

It didn't last. A few weeks later, Amelia Dyer was at their door. She begged Arthur and Polly to let her come and live with them. They could not turn her away. She was agitated and said she needed money. Looking round at her daughter's lovely home with its fashionable furniture and nice ornaments, she wondered how they had so much. She told them without shame or embarrassment that she needed to borrow from them, she was in debt but she would pay the money back when everything was straight. Polly's heart sank as Arthur sold off the contents of their new home to raise the money. He reassured her they would be fine, it would all work out. He mentioned in passing that his employer was not doing so well, business was poor, so he'd been let go, himself. He could live on the money they raised from their belongings and seemed to relax into the situation, not worried about work or income or bills. They would all be fine, he told his wife, fine.

And so the baby business began again, Dyer bringing women into Arthur and Polly's home for their confinement, conducting the business she knew so well, delivering babies. By the time they had been married for six months, the Palmers provided a home to Dyer, Annie, Alfred and Lily; in addition there were women who came in for their confinements and four babies waiting for adoption. Arthur sat back and watched the money come in, eighty pounds here, forty there, another thirty for an adoption and so on. He did not have to look for work with this going on around him and he settled into a quiet lazy life being kept by the baby farming business. He would be asked to plead guilty or not guilty to aiding and abetting Amelia Dyer's crimes when he arrived in court, but he felt he had only sat back and watched. Innocent Arthur, who only lived off a baby farmer's earnings.

But, still, for all the money that came in they were poor and could not rise out of their poverty. Things were hard, they struggled along.

Amelia Dyer suffered from another breakdown that year. She was taken away to another asylum, under an order that described her as distressed and incoherent. Arthur and Polly were left, in their first married home, with hardly any furniture, little money and seven children to care for. Very quickly, they set about getting themselves straight and went to stay with Arthur's mother. They arrived there without any of the children. Arthur had taken them all: Annie, Alfred and Lily plus the four "adopted" babies to the door of Barton Regis Workhouse, where he had left them and disappeared. They were taken in, on the charity of the parish and cared for.

Polly did not realise where these children had all gone. She found it hard to accept Arthur's story that they had gone to live with the mothers who adopted Dyer's babies from time to time. They argued but his unrelenting logic in the quarrel and the firm repetition of the names of women she'd dealt with eventually wore her down. She was confused as he mentioned the names and places, some in London, some in Reading, others she did not know. Polly didn't know that her siblings had been discarded so easily, she had lived with them during the last ten years; she chose to believe him and learn to live without them. She experienced no remorse. It turned out that one of the babies died in the workhouse; the death was recorded as similar to those of many babies in Dyer's care, malnourished, undersized, listless and unresponsive. Another two of the abandoned children had the good fortune to be reunited with their mothers, who still lived in the area; being adopted had not taken them very far from home.

Arthur and Polly then had time to take stock, stay with his mother for a while and decide on their next steps.

Chapter 9: A girl called Queenie

May 1895

It was inevitable that Polly and Arthur would go on living as they had before. His mother-in-law was out of their lives for the time being, so Arthur became pro-active in looking for potential adoptions. Where Dyer had written her advertisements and letters with a tone of formality and respectability, Arthur became the well-bred gentleman looking for a child to give a good life. He and Polly took on the role of a respectable married couple, who, unable to have children of their own, looked for adoptable (legitimate) children. Arthur used his usual charm and his way with words to compose advertisements which would attract more genteel clients, who would pay well and expect confidentiality in return. Arthur also made it clear that any adoption would be supported by agreements drawn up by solicitors, legitimising the arrangement before it had even taken place. Once the adverts were sent to the printer and the letters drafted in his rakish hand, they sat back and waited for their clients to arrive.

Quite soon, Polly was putting on her smart cloak and bonnet and going to meet women desperate to give their children to homes where they could be cared for, if not loved. Polly didn't have her mother's skills as a midwife to provide the confinement homes for women to have their babies, but with her well-dressed husband with his easy manner and affectionate air beside her, she came home with babies to care for and bank-notes to stuff into her own apron pockets. So, Arthur and Polly brought in plenty of money and their hard times seemed to be behind them.

Polly was experienced in sorting through hand-sewn napkins and knitted baby clothes, identifying those which would fetch a price at the pawn shop and which would service as clothing for the wasting little infants in her home. She didn't know as much as her mother about "the quiet" brought on by the powders she could have given to the babies to help them fade away quietly till she could make take their little bodies to some sluice or stream. She would not bother with death certificates; death certificates had got her mother into trouble long ago and had led to a prison sentence. No, Polly had to harden herself to carry out that role. She managed.

Arthur saw to the agreements, signed by solicitors to give the proceedings a legal air. There were dozens of receipts, evidencing very large amounts of money he had received in exchange for the children who disappeared. When the police finally came for him, they found these papers in his belongings. However, without bodies to confirm that the children had been taken and killed they could not make use of this evidence. There was only one that could be accounted for, a little girl called Queenie Baker.

Queenie was four years old, healthy and strong. She was tall for her age and well turned out. Arthur communicated with her family in Bristol and went off to collect the child with adoption papers all in order. For a while, he thought it would be nice for Polly to have an older child, a companion who might fill the gap left by Lilly and Annie. Polly thought she would like to walk in the parks and gardens with her childish companion; they might wear matching ribbons on their bonnets or have the same trim on their cloaks and gloves. She was used to admiring glances from the Sunday walkers, who always thought she and her husband made a handsome couple. Now she imagined the same admiring looks, especially when Arthur would join them and they made the picture of a happy family. Polly's imaginings did not last long; they were soon on the move again.

Queenie remembered the excitement of Bristol Temple Meads station. There was noise all around them, the sounds of people calling out to each other, the slamming of train doors and the shrill blasts of whistles. The huge trains belched out smoke and steam, the air was prickly with the sooty smuts that irritated her eyes. Her "mother" and "father" bustled her along, telling her they were going to the seaside, Queenie didn't really know what they meant. They met up with a huge, tall lady, taller than any lady Queenie had seen before. "This is your grandmother." She was told. She thought it must be true if these people were, now, her parents. The family she'd known up till now was becoming a vague memory, it was all so confusing. Queenie looked into the stern face of the tall woman. She could see no warmth there, did not sense any affection. However, she saw the woman embrace the adults, stiffly and bid them goodbye. They climbed into the train and waved at the woman until she became a distant figure, standing head and shoulders above the others on the platform.

As the train rattled and shook its way towards Plymouth, Queenie listened to "father" talking about the sea and the ships he had sailed on. She heard his boastful voice talking about how successful he had been at sea and the things he might have done. The carriage rocked gently and rhythmically and Queenie slept until they reached the coast. In a rush of sea and boats and carriages, they ended their journey, arriving at a house in a place called Dartmouth. They moved into a little cottage, owned by a Mrs Barber who was the landlady. Mrs Barber was impressed by the couple, who gave their names as Mr and Mrs Patson. She noticed how well dressed they were, saw the quality of their polished boots and well made clothes; she knew them to be educated and poised. She always asked her guests a few questions about themselves, it was a sensible precaution when some would flit without paying and others damaged her property. Most of her clients were retired seamen who did little harm to anyone and wanted quiet lives. She was curious about this couple and their child. Mr Patson told her he was a Scotland Yard detective in Dartmouth on business, so he asked her not to draw attention to them. The wife remained quiet when her husband answered her questions, nodding in agreement at everything he said. The little girl told them her name was Queenie, "Victoria!" the man corrected her. She grew quiet at his intervention, skipping up the steps and looking out to the sea. They took the little girl inside and settled into the cottage.

As the week progressed, Mrs Barber saw the couple going out and about. They still walked with the grace she had first noticed. They walked along the sea front, looking at the boats and ships, nodding to passers by. They were like any holiday makers she had seen. She saw them going into tea shops and public houses, though they did not seem to be drinkers. They kept themselves to themselves. They visited many local businesses and ordered items on approval or on trial and goods were delivered to the cottage. Mrs Barber was curious, but Patson reminded her of their sensitive situation, he gave her a wink and walked off. But what she also noticed was that the girl did not come out of the house. She seemed to be kept in all day long which surprised the landlady, after all, children loved being near the sea.

"Is the little girl unwell?" she asked the couple, who were setting out for a walk.

The woman stayed quiet, deferring to her husband. He drew Mrs Barber aside, as if there were eavesdroppers waiting to hear his every word. "Mrs Barber," he confided, "you'll remember I told you about my job?" He raised an eyebrow and looked at her intensely.

"Well, yes…"

"You see, little Victoria is part of an investigation I'm involved with. We're here keeping a low profile for a short while. Later on in the week, I'll need to take her to Manchester, where she'll make an important contribution to a major case. I cannot say any more!" He paused, as if to make sure she realised that he was serious. "But if you keep an eye on the papers, you'll find out all about it. Meanwhile, she's safe and sound inside and we are looking after her."

She felt as if she had been put in her place, though he had done it gently as he had confided his serious business to her. She let them go on their way. Later in the week when she saw the man leaving with the little girl, she thought he might be taking her to Manchester. The girl was well turned out, looked healthy and lively, so she did not worry any more.

What she didn't know was that he had woken Queenie up that morning, telling her they were going on a trip to the sea. The little girl had been excited, fed up of being imprisoned in the cottage with only bread and water for her food. She helped her "mother" get her dressed and stayed still while she brushed her hair. She chatted happily as they got ready for the outing. She asked if mother would be joining them but was told she would be packing for their journey home. She took "father's" hand and they set off. Arthur told his wife to start packing as they would be leaving soon. He led the little girl through the streets of Dartmouth. She looked around in delight and amazement at this strange place, there was a bustle around the shops and she saw other children excitedly playing and laughing, enjoying their holiday. She asked him to slow down, he was walking rather fast. They came to a place in the middle of the town and he let go of her hand. "You must wait here, Queenie," he said, "I have to do something, stay here, children aren't allowed. I will be back for you in a few minutes."

Arthur then went off for the day, Polly never knew how he had spent that day, it was dark when he returned and Queenie was not with him. He told her he had found someone to take the child. She was sad; she thought they could have kept Queenie, as her mother had kept some of the little ones she'd taken in. Polly had no child of her own and had wanted Queenie to be her special little companion. Arthur calmed her - there would be other little ones for her to care for. They would get a tidy amount for Queenie's little things; he encouraged her to pack them all carefully. He calmed her fretting and cooed his flattering praise for her good looks and sensible way of looking after him. Over the next few days, she packed their things carefully.

That morning in Dartmouth, Queenie had stayed quietly waiting for her "father" to return. She stood, for a while, looking in a baker's window. The bread and buns made her mouth water and she realised she was hungry. The baker came and shooed her away from the shop. She didn't look like the usual beggars who lingered at his door waiting for stale bread or buns, but she was not good for his business anyway. She wandered towards the corner, hoping to catch a glimpse of Arthur when he returned for her. She grew tired, so she sat on a wall outside a church and watched the world go by. She needed to go to the toilet and cried when she wet herself, but no one seemed to notice. The day went by and she was sad and abandoned, but still, she thought he would be back for her.

A kind woman stopped and spoke to the child: "Have you been here all day?"

Queenie nodded, she thought she must have been.

"Where are your mother and father?"

"Father told me to wait here; he's coming back for me."

"But you were here this morning when I went to work and you are still here now. Where is he?"

Queenie couldn't say, but a big tear found its way down her cheek and she began to sob. The woman took her hand, "Come on dearie, and let's get you sorted. Oh dear, look you've spoiled your lovely dress. I bet you're hungry, too."

Queenie nodded and let the woman lead her. She took her to the police station where the desk sergeant found her something to eat, hot sweet tea and a thick slab of buttery bread. Queenie perked up. Her wet things were taken away and she was swaddled in a big, scratchy blanket. She felt better when she was eating and they asked her lots of questions. Queenie couldn't answer them all, everything had been so strange. So much had happened in such a short time. She knew her name was Queenie Baker, some people called her Victoria. She was four years old, but could not remember her birthday. She knew her real mother but hadn't seen her for a while. She had a new mother and father and they were named...Patson. They were a fine lady and gentleman with lovely clothes and things and they smelled nice, like flowers and perfume. She could not tell the police their address but they were staying at the seaside. They had a nice place to stay, with a cosy bed and nice chairs but she didn't know where it was. It was near some boats, she could see them from the window. She had to stay in that room even though she would have liked to go out to see the boats close up. They had left her on her own, she said, and she was hungry. They gave her bread and water but she did like cheese and pie, did they have any pie here? The policeman said he would look for some.

There was not enough information for the police to return her to her family. They pressed. Did she know where they came from? Oh yes, they came on a train. And where had they started the journey? At a big station with lots of trains and smoke in the air. Is there anyone who could look after you? Queenie didn't know. Do you have any brothers or sisters? Aunts or uncles? Maybe a grandmother or grandfather? She suddenly remembered the grandmother who had waved them off at the station and began to describe her. She could not tell them anything to help; only that she was tall and she was waving.

While they pieced the story together they searched for clues, almost every house in Dartmouth could boast a view of a boat or two. The name Patson was not familiar to the police. An officer took Queenie to an orphanage and asked them to take her in for the time being, they did not know whether they would ever find anyone for her or not. It was likely she wouldn't stay at the orphanage for long, the workhouse was the proper place for an abandoned child like this, but the kind sergeant hoped they would keep her; she'd have a better chance there.

The following morning, the police sent officers out to look for witnesses and put together a description of the Patsons. Someone suggested they try the rented cottages along the sea front and they headed to Gloucester Cottages. Next day, they spoke to Mrs Barber who told them all she knew. The police were late, the Patsons had been gone a couple of days. She described the couple and their behaviour. The day they'd left, Patson spoke to her himself, Mrs Patson had stayed at the end of the path. She'd noticed they had lots of luggage, it seemed more than they had brought with them. Then she had realised what they had done, parcels and packages continued to arrive at the cottage. There were bills left unpaid and demands for money coming to her home from all over the country. Distressed as she was about the bills and goods arriving, Mrs Barber was mainly concerned about the child. She had known there was something strange and she told the police about how they had kept the child inside all the time they were there. She told them that he was a Scotland Yard detective and they all knew - as she said it - that it was not true.

The police issued a warrant for the arrest of the man who had abandoned the child in Dartmouth. By this time, Arthur and Polly were long gone. They had headed back to Bristol. Once there they decided to carry on moving and change address once more. They went on to Cardiff and settled there for a while. There was not much the police could do now, but a little article was written up for the *Police Gazette*. Some of the detectives who read the account thought it reminded them of Arthur Palmer.

Chapter 10: Anderson is involved

March 1896

Anderson felt the bite of the cold March morning. He hurried his pace to stay warm and kept his head down, into the wind on the way to work. The air was fresh, the smells of the night soil and the filthy river receded as the light began to spread across the sky. At least it wasn't raining; at least his coat would not be steaming and damp all day in the station. There weren't many people about as he reached the station, the odd early morning walker heading to work or delivering a package, no one to catch his attention really.

It was quiet when he got in to work; it usually was at this time of morning. There would be a few drunks or burglars in the cells downstairs, maybe a vagrant who'd needed a bed for the night had found his way there, but it would be quiet, that was for sure.

Suddenly, there was a rush of activity as PC Barnett heaved himself through the station door. The constable was flushed and panting, he was obviously distraught. Anderson noticed he was struggling under the weight of a sack slung over his shoulder. Barnett stood by the sergeant's desk and gasped for breath.

Everyone waited. Barnett's breath grew more normal, more regular. His face was still flushed as if he'd been running for a long time; this was also the face of a man in distress. He heaved the sack onto the counter. As it landed with a dull thump, water oozed from it, and the onlookers stepped back instinctively. Everyone looked.

"What is it?" Anderson asked. "What's happened?"

Barnett struggled to speak, but finally managed to reply, "Looks like a child, found in the river this morning."

"All right, Barnett. Go and take your coat off. Someone get this man some tea. Let's take this to the mortuary and have it examined properly."

People began to move, someone took Barnett's coat and he sat in the back office. The sack remained where it lay, Anderson caught the custody officer's eye and the nod of his head indicated he should move it for the moment.

The experienced detective knew they'd have to ask some big questions to get moving on this quickly. By the size of it, it had to be a small child. Enough little infant bodies were found in the shallows of the river, in bins, in alleys to show how their lives were held cheaply and often shamefully. He would work hard to find out what had happened here, he hated the way young women were forced to dispose of children - some through illegal abortions, many "accidentally" rolling over and suffocating the babies in their beds and so many emaciated babies who had not been nourished or were dosed with sleeping powders – "the quiet"- to keep them secret. He felt a catch in his throat as the emotion began to rise, emotion for his own dead babies and his poor wife who mourned each still-born life, each painful miscarriage. For them, life was not cheap, it was the most precious gift that eluded their little home. He'd get to the bottom of this.

Anderson sent an officer to get the local surgeon to meet him in the mortuary. He spoke to the desk sergeant to find out when Barnett had gone out on duty. He learned that a man had run into the station very early that morning. They found his name in the station ledger, Charles Humphreys. This man had told the young constable that he'd found a body in the river, he kept saying "parcel" and was obviously upset. Barnett had gone with him to the riverside; the sergeant said he was a bargeman, so they assumed it was to his boat. As Barnett had left, the sergeant had found the sack and thrust it into his hands, thinking he'd have to bring this parcel back with him. Everyone who was listening nodded and muttered things like "too right" and "well done." They'd gone off together and Anderson had seen what had happened next.

Anderson dispatched all available officers to go along the river bank and see if they could find any clues or witnesses. He sent another detective to find Humphreys and bring him in to hear his story. Then he went to speak to Barnett.

Barnett was calmer, by now. He was still shaken and upset. But he was able to tell the detective that he'd gone to the river with Humphreys and seen the parcel lying in the boat. He'd seen the soggy brown paper around the lumpy bundle and glimpsed what Humphreys had seen, a bolt of dark stuff covering a tiny foot and a little glimpse of leg. He and Humphreys had bundled it into the sack and he'd run back to the station. Anderson asked where Humphreys was now and was relieved to hear he was still at the place where the body had been found. Barnett knew he was local, a relief to Anderson. He knew he didn't have to go looking all round the rivers and canals of England to find him. He asked if Barnett had written anything down and knew he had to do it when he felt ready.

"Will you come with me when the surgeon arrives?"

"Do you think I sh..." his voice trailed off.

"Yes, I think it should be you." Anderson knew the PC should be there, to lay his ghosts, to finish what he had begun, it wasn't going to be easy, but would be the right thing.

Within the hour, the surgeon, William Maurice, arrived and they all went to the mortuary, a cold windowless room beneath the cottage hospital. Barnett had composed himself and walked steadily along beside them. Anderson congratulated himself that the sack had been dispatched ahead of them, Barnett wouldn't have to heave it over his shoulder again or feel its damp weight. As they walked, Dr Maurice made comments which matched Anderson's thoughts - life was cheap, the bodies of illegitimate babies turned up in all kinds of places. The doctor despaired of the number of certificates he'd had to sign and now he had to record another death, adding to the infant mortality figures.

Inside the mortuary, they approached the parcel on the table. Maurice was concerned with the method of death, Anderson looking at every possible way of finding clues. The doctor began to unwrap the bundle. The first layer was brown paper, which made it just like any other parcel, tied with some macramé string. Inside they saw the flannel fabric that Barnett had described, it was obviously a piece of infant clothing, most likely a shawl. As the next layers were removed the body of a baby girl was revealed. Anderson watched each layer as it was pulled back; he saw each one as a possible clue. There was more flannel material, newspaper and some baby's napkins. Wrapped up with all of these and with the little dead body was a house brick, the weight intended to make sure she would not be found. Once the child was revealed, there was one unmistakable detail that none of them missed. The little girl's face was frozen in a horrible pose, the eyes protruding in a way that was consistent with her being strangled. Around her neck was a piece of tape, white tape used in dressmaking, wrapped twice around her throat and tied neatly below her ear, this tape had stopped her breath. They recorded the date of death, 30th March 1896. In a grim and ghoulish pantomime they posed for the photographer who recorded their presence and the state of the little girl's body for the records – a new-fangled addition to the work of the police. Maurice was sure that she'd been dead for some time; there was a stench about her, stronger than the river.

Later that day Anderson went down to the river to speak to Humphreys and find out the story in full. The day had remained cold, but it was bright, now, and the countryside had a sharp, clear beauty. He'd left a dazed and exhausted Barnett at the station, writing his notes up in his clumsy joined script. He walked along the path with

Sergeant Harry James. Of all the officers he worked with, he knew James was as meticulous as he was. He knew James as honourable and just. Walking along the river bank, Anderson felt that everything about him was as neat and sharp as his wit and keen eye for detail. The two walked in silence, allowing one another to take in the scene. There were signs of the growing town of Reading, of gasworks and factories and the sprawl of houses. In the fields that reached away from the river there was little to see, the trees along the bank were beginning to put out green shoots for the coming spring. In places the water was slow-moving and calm; by the weirs it gushed and splashed in its noisy journey. The further they moved from town, the harder the towpath became: rutted and bumpy under-foot, where horses had left their mark in the winter mud.

They found Humphreys sitting on his boat. It was a common narrow-boat, the type that travelled up and down here every day, bringing cargo to the town and materials to the factories. They saw a calm, quiet man who was thinking about what had happened to him that day.

Anderson and James stopped beside the barge. They didn't need to introduce themselves. James was in uniform and the bargeman had been expecting them. They greeted one another silently. James indicated the narrow-boat, "What you carrying?" he asked.

Humphreys spoke gently, "Ballast," he told them, "for the railway buildings." Silence fell again. Humphreys climbed down to join them on the path.

"I suppose you want to see where I found it!" A mock boldness came into his tone; he was sorely troubled by the whole affair. He took them to a spot quite close to the bank, where the water was shallow. He pointed to the place where he'd seen the parcel. He explained that he'd had to use a boat hook to pull it in; did they need the hook as evidence? They thought not. They looked at him curiously and he said, "I know, I know! It looks like I'm greedy or something, but I was curious. You don't often see things like this here in the water."

"What did you think it was?" Anderson was curious to know.

"To be honest, I thought it was a parcel of cloth, thought I could get some use out of it, or sell it to someone who could."

He went on to describe how he'd pulled the parcel in and found it was not completely waterlogged. He'd started to open it before he realised the contents were human, he'd seen the tiny limb. That was when he'd run to the police station.

There was not much more to tell them, he thought he should get on his way. "Ballast to deliver!" he told them, as if that was important now. They thanked him, and James shook him firmly by the hand. A wave of sadness crossed his face, and he began, "Did you...?"

"Yes." said James, emphatically, "a little girl. We'll be in touch, Mr Humphreys. We may need to talk to you again. Thanks you for your help."

They watched him return to his boat and began their walk back to the station. Their pace may have been a little slower now and they still did not speak very much on the way.

Anderson's mind was working hard; he needed to find more evidence. He needed to start finding clues to put together. Harry James was thinking he'd send Barnett home, let the young constable get some rest; give him a chance to play with his own little girl before she went to bed.

Chapter 11: Closing in

April 1896

They had Dyer in custody; they wanted to charge the daughter and son-in-law for murder and for being accessories to the Ogress' crimes. The police were under pressure, there was an urgency about the way they had to build the whole case so no jury would be left in any doubt about the guilt of these monsters. Anderson shivered when he thought that they had not been able to proceed until they had a body but was comforted by the knowledge that the search was on.

He went to his superiors and asked for more officers and more resources to bring all this evidence together. His bosses allowed him to use his time and his team to do what they needed. He told them of his frustration, explained that he and his men were worried they would not make the case against Dyer and her accomplices stick. The worst scenario they imagined was that Dyer and her family would walk free and disappear, never to be brought to justice again.

Anderson's Chief Inspector called him in: "Have you heard of George Tewsley?" he asked.

Anderson had not.

"Well I hope you won't be put out, Detective Constable, but he's being given the job of bringing this case to court. He's well connected and has a great reputation for getting things done. He'll be here this afternoon and wants to meet with as many officers as he can; there'll be some coming from London and some from Reading. I understand he has officers on their way to Bristol and Cheltenham already. You're to work with him, let him use your knowledge and insight into Dyer and her lot. You all right with that?"

Anderson realised this was his time to object, claim the case was his and have a tantrum about the loss of fame and reputation if he wanted but that was not his style or his intention. "Of course, Sir." His reply was humble, earnest. "I'll make sure he has access to everything we have and he can work with any of the men involved in this case. Sir, I want her convicted. I want an end to the trail of death she leaves behind her."

The senior officer looked into the face of the man who had been so determined in his pursuit of Dyer and her crimes. He had seen Anderson's face frozen in the photograph taken with the first little victim's body; he guessed that moment and the moment of Dyer's arrest would always be frozen in time for James Anderson. He was a good officer with strong convictions and he would be an asset to the team that Chief Superintendent Tewsley put together. Anderson would help in any way he could; he had a deep conviction and was always professional in his conduct. The Inspector had faith in Anderson and firmly believed that this case would be successful with such strong and loyal police officers involved.

"You know, Sir, when a prostitute is murdered in London, there's a frenzy and an outcry. But this woman could be responsible for dozens of lives, but because they're babies, infants…"

"Good work, Anderson, we'll be meeting Tewsley here at one. I'll expect to see you at the meeting. Ask the desk sergeant to set up the briefing room; there will be a lot of people coming. Tell Sergeant James to be there, too. "

"James has a day off, Sir."

"Get him a message, ask him to come."

"Yes, sir."

Anderson made to leave, saluting his senior officer. As he turned, the inspector stopped him in his tracks, "Oh and Anderson…"

"Sir?"

"Good work. You've been doing a great job here. I want you to know your work has not been overlooked."

"Thank you, Sir." He hurried out to prepare for the meeting.

At one that afternoon, the meeting room was packed with police officers from Berkshire, London, Bristol and Gloucestershire, all places involved in the story of Dyer's murderous history. Anderson was invited to the front of the room, to join his Chief Inspector and other senior officers he had not met before. A photographer was setting up his tripod and his clumsy, complicated equipment. Cases of papers were being carried into the room and there were officers already working their way through them. Bags of evidence were being unpacked onto a table at the front; Anderson shuddered at the sight of the holdall that had held the little body, the brick that had weighted it, the strings that had held the parcel shut and the tape, the awful white tape used to strangle the infants. When George Tewsley arrived, everyone in the room looked around. He was a large, rotund figure who wore a coat, buttoned to the throat and a bowler hat which seemed to balance on his head. He was tall and filled the room with his obvious presence. His handlebar moustache was impressive and added to his authoritarian air. His expression was serious and purposeful. He looked every bit the man who would get things done. Tewsley introduced some of the people in the room and mentioned that many of them had made significant contributions. He mentioned Anderson and James by name and Anderson was proud to have been recognised. He called them to the table and asked the photographer to take a picture of himself and the two officers standing at the table where the evidence sat. Harry James appeared, dressed in his Sunday suit, he had not had time to put on his uniform when he had received the message calling him to attend the meeting. Their images were captured for history to recall the officers who were on the trail of the already notorious baby farmer.

Tewsley then introduced a civilian, Mr Bennett from the NSPCC who had made a significant contribution in explaining the crimes and the way they fitted in with the horrors of child neglect; he mentioned that Bennett had also had dealings with the Dyer household. He explained that Mrs Bennett had had dealings with Amelia Dyer's companion, Jane Smith. Anderson and James knew her as the mousy woman sitting in the corner, by the fireplace, on the day of the arrest. They had never really understood her role in the murders, nor had they managed to make a case against her. Bennett stepped forward to inform the assembly that his wife had gone to look for Jane "Granny" Smith. She had been unable to find her at first, then heard that Smith was so worried, so unable to cope that she had gone back to Barton Regis workhouse and begged to be taken back to live there. It seemed she wanted to end her days there, away from the strangeness of the life she had led with the Dyer family. They would carry on speaking to her and adding to her testimony, she must be able to corroborate much of what they were piecing together about the comings and goings in that house.

Tewsley set to the work in hand. He had already decided the areas he needed to concentrate on. He spoke directly and each point he made went straight to the task in hand. They had to put this case together as quickly as possible. He allocated officers to go and find everything and anything they could to tie the Palmers to the murders. He sent some to Willesden, where the Palmers had once lived, to find any information they could. They were to question the neighbours and look for any witnesses they could find. He asked them to follow up a witness who had helped an older woman carry a heavy bundle from a bus. Could that bundle have been an infant body? He instructed them to go back to the landlord and landlady and check the house bricks from their yard. Were they the same as the ones in the bag in the river, the second bag they had found containing the bodies of Doris Marmon and Harry Simmons? They would also need to ask the landlady about the little tooled-leather boots she had been given as a gift; they must be able to find out the story behind them. Tewsley was serious, stern in his instruction, all the evidence had to be secure, clear and unquestionable.

He dispatched other teams to go back to Cheltenham, Bristol and other addresses in Caversham and Reading. They all knew that Dyer's ability to stay one or more steps ahead of the law was down to her constantly being on the move. They needed to trace the names of mothers who had agreed to adoptions, he reminded them to look for details like the clothes the children had been left with, he was particularly interested in a fawn coloured knitted garment, which should have been easy to identify. He reminded them to check and recheck the pawn tickets and the vaccination certificates they had found among Dyer's papers. This was going to be intense and demanded a huge amount of man-power. Tewsley acknowledged the help he needed from so many forces.

The room was becoming hot, there were officers standing, shuffling their feet. Tewsley did not stop delivering his message, even though he was aware of their discomfort. He allocated other teams to visit pawn-shops in the local area and see what had been "popped" and if any items had been redeemed.

He encouraged the local team to continue searching the river and its banks for more bodies; since the first one had been found they had discovered the second bundle containing two babies. There may be more. He warned them to prepare themselves to find many bodies and see many horrors.

He moved on to talk about Dyer herself, she was safe in custody and would be moved from Reading Gaol to London for her trial. They were keeping her under close guard. She had threatened to take her own life before now; he was scathing when he mentioned an attempt to strangle herself in the same fashion as the babies with a shoe lace and of previously immersing herself in puddles to try and drown. A few sniggers and whisperings went around the room, but he called the audience back to seriousness. He reminded them, sternly, that they wanted this trial to be a success. They had to stay focused on the task. What he was saying had a serious message; it was likely that Dyer would plead insanity. He told them that there was documentary evidence that she had been held in asylums and treated as an inmate there. They had to be sure she was not going to get away with an insanity plea. He went on to talk about the records which would be used in court to say she had suicidal tendencies and used opiates to medicate herself. As he spoke, the officers in the room became serious and knew the onus was on them to make sure the case was strong enough to get the result they desired.

He began to draw his remarks to a conclusion informing the officers in front of him that legal teams were going into the institutions to check the records to see whether there had been any substance to her insanity or whether they could prove she was creating a web of deceit. He mentioned, too, that he had people looking into her time as a nurse and whether she may have learned a few tricks along the way. He was also in contact with the place she had served her prison sentence for "child cruelty" all those years ago, but first reports were indicating that she had been a model prisoner. He was going to ask the Bristol police to check on her family, whoever was still willing to talk to them, about her girlhood experiences nursing her mother through her madness.

"I think you'll agree," he looked up and fixed some of the men in the room with his firm stare, "we're serious about this case. I am determined to make sure that Dyer is not able to get away with these crimes. I am putting much of the case into your hands. I trust you to do your best to help me secure this conviction on behalf of the children, their families and the officers who have helped to uncover her crimes. This is a distressing case, you'll all agree. I thank you for your help."

Feet shuffled in the room as the assembly began to disperse, the officers getting ready to go about their work. Anderson was impressed; he was filled with hope that this Superintendent would make it work and help seal the case against Amelia Dyer.

"Before you go," the room became hushed; Tewsley had something else to say, "I need evidence against Arthur Palmer. It's been like his mother-in-law's case - we have evidence of adoptions going on, we have hearsay evidence from neighbours and the like, but we do not have a body or a complainant to speak out against him or his wife. Keep your ears to the ground. Thank you for your time and attention."

Chairs scraped the floors, feet stomped towards the doors, the men were mobilised into action, to go and find whatever they could to bring the case to its fitting end. A young officer, Anderson thought his name was Greg, came sheepishly to the front. Tewsley looked at him as if he were some kind of specimen, a piece of evidence himself. "Excuse me, Superintendent," he spoke, quietly and calmly, "I was listening to you there, when you talked about Palmer. I was reminded of a little piece in the *Police Gazette* a while back. It was a story about a little girl abandoned by a dandyish man in some seaside place. I wondered…"

Tewsley was immediately interested; he turned and gave the young policeman his full attention.

"Can you remember when you read this? Where it was?" And even before the young man could answer, he was beckoning one of his men to come and listen and get this all written down. When Greg had nothing to add, he sent the two men off to look into the story. Tewsley spoke to the few left in the room, Anderson, James and their Chief Inspector included: "When they have some more information on this one, I'll have it followed up. We need something, anything to wipe the smug grin off Arthur Palmer's face."

75

Chapter 12: First Confession

April 1896

Albert Ward heaved himself from his chair and checked his watch. It was time for his last round before his shift finished, he would check on all the detainees and be sure to look in on the condemned cells. It was growing light very early and promised to be a mild morning. He'd go home, eat some of last night's supper, check on his vegetable patch and crawl into bed. It was not so easy to fall asleep on a lovely spring morning but the bed would be warm where Rosie had slept before getting up for her shift in the pickle factory. Albert sighed, he was getting too old for this life, really, but it was a good job and had supported him well as his family grew and went off into the world. He'd never had to do the back-breaking farm work his father had done, nor the mundane jobs like Rosie and his brothers in factories and in the railway yards. It was no hardship for him to leave the comfort of the officers' room and begin his morning rounds.

He loved this building; it was not like other prisons, it didn't look like a barrack block. This was an architect designed building with separate cells for every prisoner, the intention was to keep them all apart. As Albert did his rounds, he looked in on various different inmates, some in for dreadful crimes, some just caught in their habitual villainous dealings. Tonight he looked in on their most famous residents, the famous writer and the notorious baby-farmer.

The writer, Wilde, had been in Reading Gaol since last May. Albert had some respect for the man. He was certainly a person of breeding and fine manners. He had never been any trouble for the prison guards and other staff. Albert knew his crime and knew of the scandal and disgust it had stirred up when the trial had taken place. But Albert had seen the worst of men and women in this gaol. He'd seen the greed and malice of some of the most intractable criminals. He didn't stand in judgement on any of them, except perhaps the other inmate he visited that night. He saw Wilde sitting at his table, writing as he always did. His body relaxed and casual as his pen scratched across the paper and Albert wondered whether he was writing poems or stories. As if he knew he was being watched, Wilde glance towards the door, Albert moved on.

When he reached the door of the cell where Amelia Dyer was being held, he shuddered. This was one prisoner he had no regard for; her crimes, although she had not stood trial yet, filled him with horror.

Everyone knew girls got themselves in trouble all the time. He knew, everybody knew, that for those girls the burden of their mistakes would mark them all their lives: they would be called fallen women, shameless hussies and the rest. He knew the babies were without blame and many a baby had been abandoned or left a foundling, as their mothers could not support them or live with the stigma of their illegitimate births. He knew families where a baby had suddenly appeared and was brought up as one of the rest; his own cousin had had a child, at sixteen years of age, and that child had been brought up as her baby sister. Very few people knew and fewer mentioned it. He'd also seen other child murderers pass thorough this place and read accounts of the trials of women who made their trade, as Dyer did, by disposing of the little mites. He'd seen stories in the papers, police reports, of babies' bodies found in drains and gutters, wrapped in rags and papers, stinking in decomposition among the rats and filth of city streets. Albert Ward did not stand in judgement on the inmates of this gaol very much, the law would see them for what they were, and justice would be done, he was just a custodian. Yet, as he stood before this cell, he felt revulsion for the woman and for her crimes.

Through the spy-hole in the door, he could see her. Although it was close to dawn, like her fellow prisoner, she was sitting upright at her table, writing.

When she'd arrived, others had commented on her appearance. She did not look like a monster, in fact she was the picture of respectability. The prison matron had been the one to take her to her cell, and reported that she was a "cool customer" whatever that meant. But Albert had a fair idea she meant that Dyer did not show emotion, did not shout out like some of the women prisoners did, nor did she want to fight with the men and women who guarded her. She was a tall woman, who held her head high and walked with dignity. Even here, looking through the spy-hole into her room, she sat with poised grace at the table where she wrote. Her hair was neatly arranged in a tight bun, her broad shoulders covered with a stylish shawl, her feet firmly planted under the table. They said that witnesses had found her easy to identify as the tall woman, like a stately ship in full sail, walking along the river bank in the early hours of the morning carrying a bundle. Shaking himself, Albert shut the spy-hole. She'd gone down the path carrying a bundle and returned empty handed and later the little bodies had been found.

Heading back to the office, Albert Ward sighed. Such sadness in the world, he thought, such a sorry state for so many innocents who would be preyed upon by evil people. He'd end his shift and head home soon.

As the morning grew lighter, Albert finished his paperwork and prepared to hand over to the morning staff, Dawkins would be in any minute to do the early shift. There was not much to report today, the night had been a quiet one. He finished his paper work and began to button his uniform jacket and straighten his tie. He heard a knocking sound coming from the corridor and went to investigate. Amelia Dyer was knocking on her cell door with something metallic, her cup, perhaps, or her plate. When Albert approached, she stopped making the noise. He opened the door and she stood back to let him come into the doorway. She was standing at her full height holding a letter in her hand. She held it out for him, and said "I have written this, it's a confession. It has to go to the court; it has to go to Tewsley. Can you see to that?"

Albert said he could and she continued; "It tells them all, whoever wants to listen, whoever needs to know…it was only me. Polly and Arthur never did anything, it was all me!"

He was taken aback by the vehemence of her words, her determined tone and her fierce glaring look. Taking the letter from her, in what must have seemed a meek way, he nodded his assent and told her it would be done. She moved from the door and he saw her glide elegantly back to the table where she'd been seated earlier that morning. There was no conversation, no pleading or begging, everything was matter-of-fact. Albert left the cell and locked the door.

When he got back to the office, Dawkins had just arrived and Miss Gibbs, the matron, was warming her hands by the fire. "Whatever is the matter?" Dawkins asked Albert, sensing his discomfort and seeing the look on his face. Arthur showed them both the note, with its neat, spidery writing in its home-made envelope. They saw it was addressed: *To the Chief Superintendant of Police*, they were interested in her choice of addressee and her spelling of the title. Without talking, Dawkins took it and unfolded the letter. The three of them gathered round and strained to read her words, making out her request to have this presented to the court and outlining her guilt with phrases like *I must relieve my mind* and *I feel my days are numbered on this earth*. They could make out her request, which confirmed what she had said to Arthur in the cell; they read on, *neither my daughter Mary Ann Palmer nor her husband Alfred Ernest Palmer I do most solemnly declare neither of them had anything at all to do with it* and stating her strong request that she, alone, *must stand before my Maker in Heaven to give a answer for it all.*

Dawkins refolded the paper so it looked as if it had not been opened. There was a silence between them, Arthur suddenly felt tired and he needed his rest after the long shift. But they all knew they had a big responsibility, to get this letter to the right people. Their instinct was to throw it on the fire, get rid of it, let the Palmers face their day in court, let the jury decide. According to the popular stories the son-in-law and daughter deserved to stand trial. Their colleagues at the court had described the hatred of the mob when Palmer had arrived, with his airs and graces to hear the charges read against him. But Ward and Dawkins were custodians of the law as well as custodians of prisoners. They knew they had to hand Dyer's confession to the police. She'd kick up enough fuss if the letter never reached the court, enough to put their jobs at risk and bring down the anger of the court too. No, they had to do the right thing. Arthur Ward smoothed his uniform jacket down, made sure the buttons were done up right and took the letter in his hands. "It's all right, Fred," he said as he put his cap on and began to leave, "I'll drop it to the police station on the way home. She's a clever one that one. She knows she hasn't got a chance now, but won't let them take her family with her. We have to trust the law, old friend, we have to trust the law."

As he left the office, out into the bright sunshine, he heard his colleague sigh and begin to rake the coals in the fire place, they'd be needed to heat up water for the morning brew soon enough. Arthur looked up to the clear, blue sky and headed for the comfort of home.

Chapter 13: Trial by jury

May 1896

When Amelia Dyer arrived for her last appearance at Reading court, she thought she knew exactly what would happen. She knew she was going to be convicted of the crimes she was charged with; she had confessed to them, hadn't she? She had written it all down to ensure that Polly and Arthur would not be implicated in any way. She was certain of their freedom. The courtroom was crowded and there were many who wanted to see her and find out what would happen to her. Some of the details of the case had already been reported in the papers and the reputation of the Ogress of Reading was being talked about in ale houses across the country, there was even a ballad sheet in circulation outlining the horrors of her tale.

She walked in head held high, her hair neatly tied up in the familiar bun. As she entered there were murmurings about her which she tried to ignore. Feet shuffled, chairs scraped the floor but she ignored all the sounds around her. She was sorry she could not see her daughter, she had hoped to reassure her that she was well and so had made an effort with her appearance. She was rather proud of the efforts she had made and the final result. She had even managed to send for her feather boa and her coat with the fur collar. But the outfit did nothing to soften her harsh features and stern expression. She looked around the court as she moved. She had not expected to see her son-in-law, safe in the belief that her confession would have secured his release and that the charges would be dropped. She looked around the courtroom for Tewsley. She spotted him standing tall and serious at the side of the court. She lunged towards him, hissing "Did you get my letter?"

He nodded, stroking his splendid moustache.

"But if you read it, why is he still here?" She pointed at Palmer, who was sitting in the dock, calm and serene as if he were watching a music hall show.

Tewsley did not respond, but could not help noticing that she was angry and put out; her plans to get the Palmers off the hook had been thwarted. He watched her take her place in the courtroom.

"Where's Polly, where's my daughter?"

"She is still in Reading Gaol, we are waiting to see what charges we can bring against her." He was emotionless, matter of fact.

"But my letter…" her voice trailed off. She knew he would not engage in this conversation any more. She allowed them to take her to the dock.

Much of what followed was procedural. As far as Amelia Dyer was concerned, it was common knowledge that she had written her confession in gaol.

When the prosecuting barrister announced that Arthur Palmer would be dismissed by the court because there was not enough evidence to secure a conviction as accessory to Dyer's murders, a gasp went around the court room. Amelia Dyer looked to see his expression change from calm detachment to smug delight. He was told to stand down, gave his mother-in-law a glance and a wink and walked to the back of the court. Dyer looked for Tewsley, who remained inscrutable, his expression never changed.

As Palmer drew level with Tewsley, the superintendent put his hand out and stopped him. Palmer was surprised, caught off guard. "Arthur Palmer," Tewsley was clear, loud, confident, "I am arresting you on the charge of abandoning a child on the streets of Devonport." Palmer's face turned grey, his confidence was shattered as he had not expected this at all and he was taken away by the officers waiting at the back of the court. Amelia Dyer, standing bewildered in the courtroom, could not have predicted what was to happen next. Arthur was taken to Devonport and charged with abandoning Queenie Baker in the street. He was found guilty and received a sentence of hard labour, just as his mother-in-law had many years before.

The trial in Reading went on without Palmer. The lawyers debated whether to admit the letters of confession as evidence and whether Mary Ann Palmer should be called to give evidence. As the talk went back and forth, Dyer tried to remain emotionless but observers noticed she was unsettled and twitchy. She could not make sense of why this was happening at all, this talk of new evidence and gathering testimony to build the case was confusing. Surely, they all knew what the outcome would be. She had confessed, hadn't she?

When the court decided to allow passages to be read aloud from her letter, Amelia Dyer showed emotion for the first time, burying her head in her hands. Miss Gibbs, the prison matron, was there to confirm that it really had been written by the defendant.

And there was another surprise for Amelia Dyer. When she heard her daughter's name called to come forward as a witness, the older woman burst into tears. Then she saw her daughter come into the court and take her place in the witness box. A court official brought in some baby clothes for the court to see. What happened next left Amelia Dyer astonished and extremely confused. Instead of helping her mother's case, Polly talked round in circles, contradicting herself in the way she told her story. When questioned about the events surrounding Doris and Harry's deaths, Polly was confused about who the babies belonged to, whether her mother was holding on to them for someone else or not, she could not be clear about some details because she was fetching coal or putting the kettle on. She was confused about the parcels and where they had been kept overnight.

The clothes presented as evidence included the little fawn coloured outfit that Evelina Marmon had identified as Doris's pelisse. Polly swore, she was adamant, that this was one that her mother had knitted for her own adopted child, Harold. Amelia Dyer looked on in disbelief as Polly gave inconsistent accounts of the events they had all lived through. If Arthur had been in court, she might have thought Polly was in his thrall, mesmerised into distorting the truth. Polly could not know about the letter her mother had sent to keep her from prosecution; Polly seemed to be trying to protect herself, but was doing it in a clumsy, ham-fisted way.

Polly was going to be kept in custody while the prosecution tried to make a case against her. She was still in court when the chairman asked Mrs Dyer to stand. Dyer was weeping openly, Polly did not look at her. The charge was read: Dyer was to go to the Central Criminal Court in London where she would be charged with the murders of Doris Marmon and Harry Simmons. They took her from the court to the train for London to be held in Holloway Prison. She tried to hold her head up high, she tried to walk with her familiar tall, sweeping gait, but she was not strong enough. She wept when the train went through places she recognised, including Clappers Bridge, where she had tried to hide some of the bodies.

Her trial took place in London two weeks later. The woman who entered the courtroom was not dressed in the showy clothes she had worn to court previously, she wore a plain black dress, as if she were in mourning for herself already. Many of the people who had helped make the case against her were called to give evidence: from Evelina Marmon and Harry's mother, Mary Ann Beattie, to the doctor who had performed the post mortems plus the Palmers' landlord and landlady. Anderson, who had worked so hard to bring this case, and even poor old Granny Smith, brought from the workhouse in her worn, white bonnet attended. Amelia Dyer stared hard at each of them as they gave their evidence, there was little new for the court to hear, most of their testimony had been referred to in Reading. Jane Smith and Evelina Marmon both avoided Amelia Dyer's gaze, too upset to let her make them falter in their tales. D C James Anderson was not intimidated by her either; he stood tall and read from his notes without a moment's hesitation. The jury listened intently, not missing a word. The case was clear-cut and everything pointed to a conviction for trafficking infants as well as the murder of the two babies.

However, the defence, as Tewsley had predicted, claimed insanity. They put the case that Dyer had been unaccountable for her actions. They tried to use her periods in asylums and the behaviour that had been recorded by her doctors to support their argument. Her barrister made much of the fact that her mother, Sarah Hobley, had suffered madness in the months before her death. Polly's testimony confirmed that her mother had been in those institutions but she made it clear that those stays had taken place at the times that parents of adopted children had come looking for her or put her under pressure. Dyer was agitated and upset as she listened while Polly gave answers which would put her insanity defence at risk. Minutes later, Polly appeared confused as she tried to remember how many children her mother had adopted, coming across as weak and muddled.

Amelia Dyer watched and listened as the daughter she had tried so hard to protect destroyed her only defence. And then as Polly stood down, and Dyer thought there could be no more surprises, she heard a call for one more witness who could discredit her insanity plea. She heard the name of someone she had not seen for many years, her brother, James Hobley. He gave his testimony confirming that Amelia was his sister but they had not seen each other for thirty-five years. When asked about his own mother's insanity, he denied it. He said she had not died a lunatic and was very clear that there was no history of madness in his family. The trial ended here. Dyer looked at her brother with disbelief and astonishment. He did not look at her, he left the court before the jury went out to deliberate.

The jury was only out for four and a half minutes – the time it took to cook an egg or strangle a baby. Their verdict was, as expected, guilty. The Ogress could not keep herself from shaking, rocking backwards and forwards on her feet. Her face was pale, her breathing shallow. The judge reached for the black cap that signalled his sentence would be a death for Amelia Dyer, the baby farmer, the Ogress of Reading.

Chapter 14: Isn't this enough?

June 1896

Sitting in the condemned cell of Newgate Prison, Dyer wrote and wrote. She had been held in this cell for three weeks, awaiting execution. Each day she washed and put on a plain dress, each day she twisted her hair into the knot high on her head which had made her recognisable to some of her victims' mothers and the witness on the path at Caversham. She told the story of her crimes and spared no detail. Her writing, small and neat, filled five journals as she accounted for her crimes and explained the way she had carried them out. Her grammar was formal, as it had been in her notes and letters, and her spelling as erratic as ever, nevertheless, it was legible and easily understood by any reader. She wrote with clarity about the babies she had strangled with the white tape, re-iterating the comment she had made after her arrest: "You'll know mine by the white tape around their necks."

The female wing of Newgate had been closed, so her cell was below the prison infirmary, close to the male wing. It was larger than the other cells, two knocked together to make the room needed for this final stay. Dyer didn't know it herself, but its previous occupant had also been a woman, condemned for the killing of a woman and her baby. The cell was warm, there were heated water pipes running along its walls. As well as the table where she was writing, the room contained a number of chairs, she was always watched by prison guards. In fact, she had five guards assigned to watch her two at a time through their eight hour shifts; there was an extra guard on duty outside the cell. The Newgate authorities recognised that she was a powerful woman and had she tried to escape they were certain they could retain her. She had not put up any such a fight.

The women who guarded her reported that, from time to time, she would sit and stare - not into space, in thought - but straight into the eyes of the wardresses. They felt her stare expressed her dislike of them; she stared at one then the other, not speaking, not betraying any particular emotion. They found this unsettling and unnerving. In fact, one of the guards was so affected by this that she asked to be removed from the detail.

In her journals she told of how she had operated her lying-in service, mentioning many of the women she had dealt with. She wrote of the little ones she had strangled and disposed of in all kinds of ways. Anyone who read her testimony could have had no doubt that she was a callous, cruel woman. She admitted her guilt in the deaths of Doris Marmon and Harry Simmons, the two babies who had been found in the river when it was searched. She claimed that she'd forgotten to mention them, even though it was the finding of these two babies' bodies that had led to her conviction. Her confession confirmed the pain and heartbreak of Evelina Marmon and Mary Ann Beattie, Harry's mother, who had lost their children and had had to identify their little bodies. She had seen them both in court; she had heard how their evidence led her closer to the gallows.

Her testimony tied in with what the police had known about her constant movement between different addresses, from Bristol to Cheltenham, Reading and Caversham in addition to a number of London addresses. She confirmed what they suspected about her movements as she travelled by train and bus between different women's houses, dropping a baby here for a few weeks to be looked after and there for so called adoptions. Travel was not cheap, the railway was popular but not within everyone's means. Anderson had often wondered where all the money had gone; Dyer should have been a wealthy woman. Now these confessions helped to show how she had paid a number of women to be her accomplices and spread some of the money in this way. Her frequent travel would also have accounted for a lot of her spending.

The message that she reinforced in her confessions was the same as the one she had tried so hard to establish in the time after her arrest. She stated very clearly that her daughter and her husband knew nothing of her crimes. She mentioned that Polly's story might have been embellished to protect her from the consequences of her actions, excusing any inconsistencies in Polly's statements. Everyone who had heard Polly in court knew that her story was full of contradictions. To all who had watched and listened, it was ironic that Dyer had worked so hard to protect her daughter but Polly had done nothing to protect her mother, rather taking every opportunity to save herself.

Her account of the way she had killed Doris and Harry was meant to absolve Polly and Arthur of any guilt. However, it betrayed a heartlessness, which even those who had investigated her crime found shocking. She admitted that the babies had been killed in Polly and Arthur's rented house in Mayo Road, Willesden. She'd carried Doris there from Reading, and stayed there overnight. It was here she killed her. She revealed that she had wrapped little Doris' body in a napkin and tucked her under the sofa where she had left her until she could dispose of her. She said that she had laid Harry on the sofa, wrapped in a plaid blanket before she "tied" him. She said she was alone, with the door locked, she said Arthur was not in the house. For a while she left Harry on the sofa, looking as though he was sleeping peacefully. Later, she placed the little boy in a holdall. To Tewsley, Anderson and others who read the confessions afterwards, the thing that stood out most was that she had the two bodies there, in Polly's house while they carried on with their lives and even went out for the evening. By all accounts, they had passed a normal evening and Dyer had slept on that sofa with the little bodies close by.

The following day, she told Polly that she had settled Doris with another family and they had gone through her clothes, sorting them for the pawn shop. Polly had liked the little beige knitted outfit and kept it to use for the little boy she had adopted, Harold.

All of this corroborated the evidence the London police had collected and made sense of some of the facts they had learned. The beige coloured outfit had been one Evelina had sent for Doris. Another witness had described how she had helped the large, older woman carry a healthy lively baby from the bus to the door of 76 Mayo Road. They could then be certain this was where Doris had been killed. The police had spoken to Mr and Mrs Culham, the landlords, and tied all the pieces of the story together. They had let the rooms to the Palmers, who had stayed there with their sickly little son. They could not have known that he was one of a stream of adopted children passing through the family's hands. Mrs Culham knew Amelia Dyer, she had often visited Polly and Arthur and sometimes stayed overnight. Mrs Culham had liked her, she seemed kind and helpful. It was Polly's mother who would pay off their rent arrears and she did remember that particular visit. The rent had been paid; little Ethel Culham, her daughter, had been admired and fussed over and Dyer had given Mrs Culham a pair of beautiful, tooled, leather boots for the child. They remembered that they had left the door unlocked that night as the Palmers and Dyer had gone out for the night. And, yes, the older woman had left in the morning carrying a bulging heavy holdall. There seemed to be little more to say. Though as an afterthought, Arthur Culham did comment that he missed some bricks from the back yard; he had been fixing the hearth and had a small pile of bricks put aside, the pile had been disturbed and one whole brick and one broken one had gone. This accounted for the bricks that weighted the holdall Dyer had put into the river before going home that evening.

She had also added comments which carried on her line of defence that she had been mentally unstable; indeed, she wondered what had stopped her killing everyone in the house in her distracted state. This did not tie in with the story of how she had put two little bundles under the settee before going out for the evening to the Sporting and Military show at Olympia.

There was enough in the confessions to bring new charges against the Palmers, charges of being accomplices and accessories to the murders. The evidence was, to the frustration of all the investigating teams, not admissible. It was a strange state of affairs that these confessions were considered to have been written by a person who was already dead. In the eyes of the law, being in the condemned cell awaiting execution made Dyer cease to be acknowledged as a living, human person. Ironically she was notified that she should appear as a witness in her own daughter's trial; the date was set for a date after her own execution. Dyer's insistence that Polly was innocent was upheld and she was never charged.

Anderson and his colleagues were downhearted, their work was not coming to the conclusion they had wanted. Chief Superintendent Tewsley shared their feelings, but continued to re-examine all the evidence before him convinced there must be some way.

The day of Amelia Dyer's execution grew near. She completed her writings, labelled the note books as her "last and true confession." On the eve of the execution she was hugely relieved to hear that the charges against Polly had been dropped. She was pleased that she had managed this much as least. That same day, a chaplain came to hear her confession and offer her words of consolation and peace. She did not have anything to say to him. The books containing everything she had wanted to say lay on the table in the condemned cell. She stood, drawing herself to her full height; she drew her shawl from the chair and wrapped it around her. The prison wardresses watched, ready to spring to the chaplain's help should they need to. However, Dyer remained calm and showed no emotion. The chaplain asked if she would like to confess. As she turned from him, ready to walk away, she indicated the place where she had been writing and said "Isn't this enough?"

There were stories that she attempted to take her own life one more time, twisting her handkerchief around her own neck and cutting off her breath. This attempt may have been as weak as some of her other attempts during her asylum stays. However, it may have been enough to make her appear groggy or dazed. She'd tried to eat some breakfast, but had not been able to, she seemed to be ill. Those who witnessed her last moments and execution did say that she seemed to collapse when the executioner, a Mr Billington, came to secure her arms with a huge, leather strap. Throughout her trial and imprisonment she had held her composure and kept a haughty dignity, it left her now. The prison guards had to hold her while her arms were restrained and supported her as she joined the little procession that left the cell.

At nine o'clock on the morning of Wednesday 10th June, 1896, she was hanged. Asked for her last words, she said, without a trace of remorse, "I have nothing to say."

Eithne Cullen was born in Dublin and moved to London when she was six years old. She writes stories and poems. She lives with her husband in East London. She is unashamedly proud of her three grown up children, and endeavours to embarrass them as often as she can.

Lightning Source UK Ltd.
Milton Keynes UK
UKOW04f0728040218
317336UK00001B/87/P